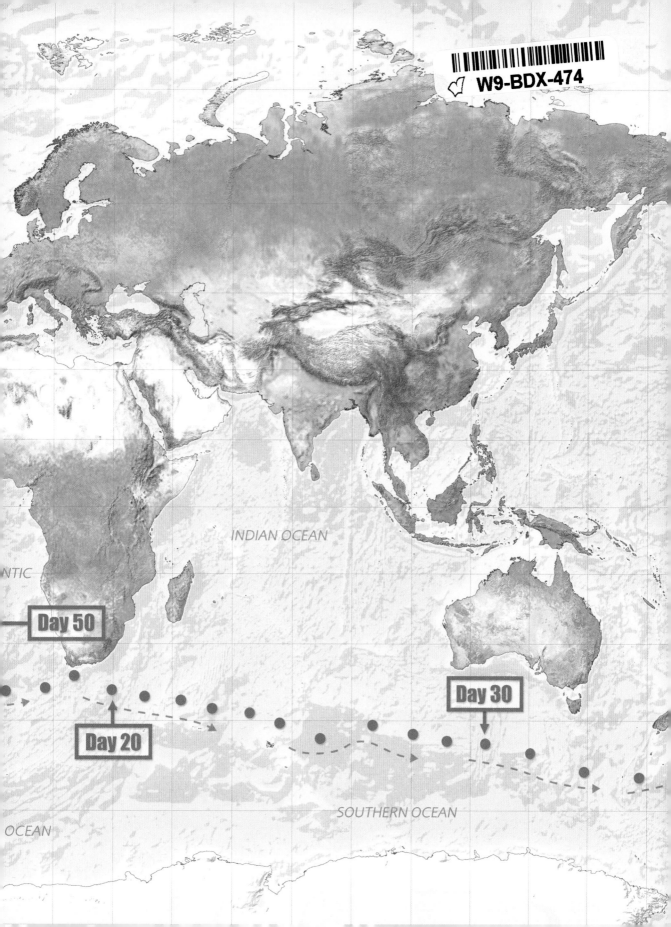

CHASING the DAWN

Nick Moloney

Photography by
Gilles Martin-Raget and Jean-Baptiste Epron

Navigator Guides Ltd
The Old Post Office, Swanton Novers
Melton Constable, Norfolk NR24 2AJ
info@navigatorguides.com
www.navigatorguides.com

ISBN 1-903872-08-1

Publishers acknowledgements: the publishers would like to thank
Orange plc for their support in the publication of this book and Nick
Moloney for introducing us to the adrenaline-filled world of ocean-
going yacht racing.

Design by Smith, Cowan and Wilkinson
Jacket design by Smith, Cowan and Wilkinson

Colour reproduction by PDQ Digital Media Solutions Ltd
Printed in Italy by Printer Trento srl

Contents

Acknowledgements

There are so many people that I wish to thank but mostly those who have supported the effort to actually compile this wad of paper and photos that reflect great memories.

When the idea was first discussed I was not very keen. I basically did not feel worthy to represent the whole team on this one. I kicked the idea around with a few friends and decided to have a go, so all of those who provided any amount of encouragement then I thank you.

I must give special mention to several people who took both me and the project under their wing and, I guess, believed enough to provide the all important ingredients... encouragement.

Special thanks to Brian Hancock for assisting with the writings, in particular the research and text for 'Le Trophée Jules Verne'. Brian is a friend and fellow sea farer who has become a writer through his will to share his life experiences and those of others. Brian has written many books about the sea, life and adventure. Thank you Brian for helping me find the words.

When I first wrote the text I passed it on to good friend and sporting journalist Edward Gorman. Ed was about to fly to New Zealand to cover the America's Cup and agreed to skim through it during his flight. At this stage the only persons that had read any text were Ed, Brian and myself and I eagerly awaited his response once in NZ. On his arrival he rang and said 'you have a book and its good'. I was relieved and flattered. I firstly sounded the text off Ed because I believe he is honest and would give me a real 'thumbs up' or down and I was very prepared for the 'thumbs down'.

Stephen Breen deserves a very special mention. Thank you for your unselfish offering of advice and contact that has been vital to the progression of this book. You have been a vital link and I will always remember and acknowledge your honest support.

To Rupert Wheeler and Navigator Guides who have constructed this book from scattered thoughts and rough text. Thank you for putting up with my impatience and for your commitment to seeing this through with me, especially unscheduled dashes to Brazil.

Thanks mum, dad, my fantastic family and girlfriend Flavie for your love and tolerance. I know that my journeys are the creator of large amounts of worry. To my closest friends, thanks for keeping me honest in life, I owe my smile to you. To my work colleagues at Offshore Challenges, my team mates and my competitors.

Thanks to all of those who helped communicate our voyage and to those who took an interest in our quest.

Thanks Orange for the chance of a lifetime. For your belief in the dream and the thrill of the chase.

On behalf of sail4cancer charity, of which I am patron, I thank you for purchasing this book as, through doing so, you have made a donation to cancer research and the assistance of helping ease the grief and sadness that accompanies this disease through events related to the sea.

To Gilles Martin-Raget and Jean-Baptiste Epron for such awesome documentation of our lives afloat through your cameras.

Finally and with every square inch of my soul... To all of my team mates, onshore and onboard, and our families. 'Merci infiniment pour votre courage et votre amitié. Que la mer berce toujours vos rêves' (Thank you for your courage and friendship. May you always dream of the sea).

Nick Moloney

I have already had many great moments in my life. I grew up with the clean sand of Victoria's south coast beaches between my toes in a small seaside town called Ocean Grove. My childhood was divided between Ocean Grove and the outer suburbs of Melbourne. My earliest and fondest memories are of the coast. I was in fact born to the sea and I owe my life to the opportunities and lessons it has given me. I guess it is fair to say that I was a surfer before I became a sailor but I have always been an adventurer and dreamer. I was first introduced to sailing by Reg Smith, our nextdoor neighbour at Ocean Grove. My father often sailed with Reg on the nearby Barwon River. Coincidentally his boat was a 20-foot/6-metre catamaran. Reg's sons and I would always be in the way when we tried to help get the boat rigged and ready for sailing. While Dad and Reg were out sailing, we ran along the water's edge yelling and cheering and trying to see how long we could keep up with the boat. Occasionally we would be taken out for a ride and I can remember the power of the boat under sail; this was a high performance, expensive racing machine, so we had to keep out of the way and move quickly. With a strong wind the boat would fly up on one hull.

Walking along the river one day, I met a man who rented out small sailboats. I found out how much they were, ran home to Mum, pleaded and made promises for several hours, begging her to lend me the money. After much nagging she finally gave in and I raced back to the boat and exchanged a year's worth of promises for an hour afloat. I had absolutely no idea how to sail, I just climbed aboard and pointed it to where I wanted to go. In a soft breeze I coasted away from the beach. Eventually I moved the sail around and started to feel the difference in power and speed with each small change. I would lie on the deck with my face close to the water, listening and watching as the water trickled past the hull. After a while I became friends with the owner and he would let me go out when he wasn't busy with paying customers. In return I helped him pack the boats away at the end of the day. I was eight years old and already becoming a professional sailor.

Our little home was about 500 metres from the waters of the Bass Strait and about 9 miles/15 kilometres from the entrance to the vast, circular Port Philip Bay south of Melbourne. Every year on 27 December a fleet of yachts would head out of the bay and cross the Bass Strait bound for Tasmania in the Melbourne–Hobart and Melbourne–Devonport races. My father had an old transistor radio that could pick up the conversations between the boats and the race organisers as they reported their positions. After watching the group of small white triangles sail out of the bay and over the horizon, we would run home and turn on the radio to listen to the transmissions. It was impossible for a young boy not to want to be one of those daring crew and to take part in the great adventure of an

ocean race. I would sail my little boat on the Barwon River, dreaming that I was in the Bass Strait racing towards Tasmania. Sometimes I would sail over to a sandbank and beach myself on my very own desert island. I had many hopes and dreams back then, and I am happy to say that a lot of them have already come true.

In 1983 *Australia II* won the America's Cup. The skipper was John Bertrand. He had taken the trophy from a team skippered by the ruthless American Dennis Conner. These two men became heroes of mine. One for achieving something that united Australia in a way that I had never seen before, and have never seen since, the other for not giving up, for holding onto his belief in himself and his crew, and for returning to regain the old Mug.

In 1995 I joined my hero, John Bertrand, on oneAustralia, off the coast of San Diego, California, USA, in search of that same emotion and victory that had united my country so many years before.

During a visit to New Zealand after the 1995 America's Cup, I found myself in the Auckland maritime museum, in a room totally devoted to the Trophée Jules Verne. This was the first time I had actually seen the

▲ The honour of sailing in the America's Cup... with my hero
© *Sharon Green*

▲ *Toshiba* upwind with the Great D.C. at the helm

© *Kos/Kos Picture Source*

trophy. I was immediately lured towards the incredible feat. Right there and then I decided that I wanted to attempt this record. In fact, I laid down three offshore sailing goals: (1) to sail around the world with a full crew; (2) to sail around the world non-stop as fast possible; and (3) to sail around the world solo.

In 1997 I joined a team skippered by Dennis Conner to compete in the legendary Whitbread Round the World Race. This was an experience that was to change my life's focus and to bring out my spirit of adventure and the real beauty of my chosen career. During my time with Dennis we raised the bar, we went where no one else had gone before on a sailing vessel. In a large storm off the Grand Banks, Newfoundland, we pushed the yacht into the record books by sailing 434.4 nautical miles in a 24-hour period. Further and faster than anyone else, ever. A thrilling experience. This was also the team that I would sail the whole way round the world with and achieve the first of three life goals, three of the greatest and most difficult tasks in the sport of offshore sailing. After the WRTWR in December 1998 I became the first person to windsurf across Bass Strait

(Bass Strait: from mainland Australia to the island state of Tazmania – 150 miles) and found out exactly where those little white triangles were heading. The journey took me 22hrs 11mins, probably one of the most physically and mentally demanding of my achievements to date, but a first and a Guinness World Record. I had been bitten by the adventure bug!

So I guess this was how I ended up lying wet and cold in the bilges of a massive ocean-going cat, surrounded by Frenchmen, acting out a dream: to set the greatest of all sailing speed records, around the world, non-stop, flat out. I had become addicted to that beautiful part of our planet that lies beyond the horizon, to the thrill of charging across the oceans on one of the biggest and fastest sailing craft in existence with a team of great sailors in search of something that did not yet exist.

But this book is not about, me, Nick Moloney. I am not a writer and never intended to have a book published about my experiences on *Orange*. It occurred to me that if I didn't tell my story this amazing adventure would not be accessible to anyone outside France. An American by the name of Cam Lewis was onboard *Commodore Explorer*, the first boat to hold the

▲ My longest day

© *Newspix/Jay Town*

Jules Verne record for circumnavigating the world in 79 days. Cam's skipper was a Frenchman by the name of Bruno Peyron, our skipper, this time under the sponsorship of Orange Communications. Cam was also the only non-Frenchman on board. He wrote a book that I have read many times, and if he had not made the effort to do this I would have never have been able to live it with him and build my own dreams and goals.

Unfortunately this recollection is through my eyes and I cannot change that. The story is basically made up of my daily logs written and sent from onboard via satellite communications and posted on my website www.nickmoloney.com. I have included extracts from my team mates' logs and character. I dearly hope that the rest of the team read and use this collection of pages as a means of reflection on an incredible race against time, an incredible moment in time.

▶ Monday 21st January 2002
Launch in Marseille. Bruno and France Rugby Team Captain Fabien Pelous smash the champagne giving our boat a new name and identity

I have two hopes for the outcome of this book.

I hope that throughout the proceeding pages you will dream, laugh maybe even shed a tear.

I hope most of all that my crew mates approve of the way I have presented OUR story and treasure this book and use it for reflection; I pray that they smile always.

This book is about 13 men with the same dream and focus who on 14 February 2002 shared the same heartache and wonder. Under the drive of a small headsail we nursed our broken dream back towards the French coast, our broken mast carving large circles in the night sky as we pitched along on a northerly course, a course that we were not due to be taking until we had exited the Southern Ocean and rounded Cape Horn.

This book is about a team! A GREAT TEAM!

TROPHÉE JULES VERNE

Le Trophée

The race to complete the fastest circumnavigation actually started more than a decade ago on a barge on the River Seine in Paris. It was an appropriate setting for a gathering of some of the sailing world's most serious contenders, among them Bruno, his younger brother Loïck, the late Sir Peter Blake, Sir Robin Knox-Johnston and Yves Le Cornec. Florence Arthaud was also there. The only other person in attendance was one of the most important: Titouan Lamazou currently held the record for the fastest circumnavigation and since the meeting was about record-breaking circumnavigations, it was only fitting that Lamazou was there.

The idea for a fastest-time circumnavigation had already been on the minds of some sailors for many years before the first formal gathering in France. It had its origins, as many do, onboard a boat, racing from Québec to St-Malo. Yves Le Cornec was no different from many sailors who find themselves with some slow time at sea. He began to daydream. Le Cornec had read Jules Verne's famous 1873 novel *Around the World in Eighty Days* and began to speculate on whether a circumnavigation under sail in less than 80 days might indeed be possible. It was a romantic notion, in theory quite possible; however, at the time there were no boats in existence that might come close to maintaining the record-setting pace needed to get around in less than 80 days. Yves knew that while at that moment in 1984 there weren't any boats capable of making the trip in the required time, the development of boats, especially multihulls, was exponential and he deemed it likely that within a few years someone would come up with the right kind of design. He put forward the idea for scrutiny, and sailors, always intrigued by outrageous possibilities, responded both positively and negatively.

The negative responses were easier to come by. At the time of Le Cornec's initial proposition, the fastest non-stop circumnavigation had been completed in 292 days. It was hardly worth comparing that trip to what was being proposed because the record was set in 1971 by the British former paratrooper Chay Blyth sailing the 'wrong way' – against the prevailing winds – around the world. He had also sailed alone and there were no crew restrictions being proposed for Le Cornec's new idea. A better example would have been the voyage of Alain Colas, a French sailor who circumnavigated in 144 days. Colas had also sailed alone and had stopped in Sydney; however, he had gone with the prevailing winds and, factoring in the extra distance sailed and taking out the time spent in port, he averaged 7.41 knots. This was still way off what was needed: a circumnavigation in under 80 days would require an average speed of between 12 and 14 knots, almost double Colas's speed.

Over time the negative responses were outweighed by more positive ones. The boats were getting faster and more seaworthy. In 1987

Frenchman Phillippe Monnet sailed a 23.5-metre trimaran around the world in 129 days with a stop in South Africa. A year later another Frenchman, a sailor whose name would in later years become entwined with the Jules Verne Trophy, shaved four days off Monnet's time. Olivier de Kersauson began his quest first to set and then to break the record.

With each new fastest time the world shrank a little in size, and the possibility of an 80-day circumnavigation began to seem more and more realistic. It started to become really feasible in 1989 when yet another French sailor, Titouan Lamazou, sailed around non-stop in just over 109 days; he won the inaugural Vendée Globe with a record time of 109 days, 8 hours and 48 minutes aboard a 60-foot/18-metre monohull. The speculation at the time was that a multihull of equal size would be able to better his time provided that the boat held together. An even larger multihull would do better, and sailing with crew would shave even more time off the record. At the time there were some 80-plus-foot/24-plus-metre catamarans racing back and forth across the Atlantic, and a cursory glance at their speeds made it obvious that if someone showed up with a well-prepared large catamaran, they should be able to better 80 days. Despite the speculation, Lamazou's record still stood when the first gathering of the Association Jules Verne took place in France.

It was late August 1990 and, while Paris baked in high-summer temperatures, Le Cornec's idea had taken hold and it was time to formalise a plan. It would be called the Trophée Jules Verne in recognition of Verne's original premise, and the rules would be simple. The start would be on an imaginary line between the Lizard, a headland at the southernmost point of Great Britain, and Ile d'Ouessant, an island off Brest on the west coast of France, circumnavigate the globe sailing south of all the great Capes, with the finish line in the same place. This line demarcates the English Channel from the Atlantic Ocean and allows competitors to set off and return to both England and France. Would-be record-setters would sail the length of the North and South Atlantic, round the Cape of Good Hope at the tip of Africa and enter the Southern Ocean, a region known for its gale force winds, gigantic waves and icebergs! Cape Leeuwin on the southwest corner of Australia was the next mark on the course albeit a cursory one, along with South Cape New Zealand, since by the time the boats passed that line of longitude they would be sailing well to the south of these island continents and heading for the real turning point of the trip, Cape Horn. At 56° 30' S Cape Horn sticks out into the Southern Ocean and marks the geographical and psychological turning point of any circumnavigation. With Cape Horn behind them sailors could look forward to a transit of the Atlantic oceans one last time before the finish. Finish in under 80 days and the Trophée Jules Verne would be yours.

To really understand the significance of the meeting in Paris one needs to understand the calibre of those in attendance. To their peers they were just well-known sailors, men and a woman who had paid their dues on the ocean racing circuit and had gained the respect of others who had also spent time at sea. What set them apart was that they had become household names in France, something that does not happen in other parts of the world. These particular sailors were the Michael Jordans and the Schumachers of the sport. Bruno was, as *Seahorse Magazine* once said, 'the best multihull sailor in the world, period'. He had set a transatlantic record in 1987 and vaulted into the limelight. Shortly thereafter his record was broken by Florence Arthaud. Not one to take such matters lightly, Peyron went out again and smashed Arthaud's record while his brother Loïck won the 3,200 mile/5,150 kilometre La Baule–Dakar race. For a while it seemed as if the brothers Peyron and Florence Arthaud owned the ocean. No one could match them and the French public loved it.

This public interest in non-stop globe girdling races originated with the first such round the world race, the Golden Globe. In 1968 nine men took part in an assortment of craft from well-worn cutters to a barely broken-in catamaran. When it was all over the race was won by a young Brit by the name of Robin Knox-Johnston sailing a little wooden double-ender. Sailing, as he put it, 'for queen and country', Knox-Johnston completed his trip in 313 days averaging 4.01 knots. He was the first person to sail single-handed, non-stop around the world, and his example has been the inspiration for many that followed. Knox-Johnston would later team up with another sailing legend, Peter Blake, to eventually set their own Jules Verne record for which both men would be knighted. Tragically Peter Blake was murdered by pirates in South America shortly before we set off on our trip around the world I was travelling in the Pyrenees when Mark Turner called and told me that Sir Peter Blake had been killed; I pulled over to the side of the road stunned by the news of the death of this sailing icon.

With these six famous sailors lending their stamp of approval to the Trophée Jules Verne, all that remained was for the first competitor to step up and attempt the challenge. By January 1993 there were three campaigns getting ready for the trip. Two of them had paid the $16,000 entry fee and declared their intensions. The third, de Kersauson, publicly announced that he would sail outside the Trophée Jules Verne format and therefore would not be paying an entry fee. He was planning the trip on his 90-foot/28-metre trimaran *Charal*. The other two entrants were, not surprisingly, Bruno Peyron, and a joint effort to be co-skippered by Peter Blake and Robin Knox-Johnston. Blake and Knox-Johnston had purchased an 80-foot/24-metre catamaran named *Formula Tag*. Blake and Knox-Johnston lengthened the boat to 85 feet/26 metres and renamed it *ENZA* for their principal sponsor, the New Zealand Apple and Pear

Marketing Board. *ENZA* was an acronym for 'Eat New Zealand Apples'.

Peyron had purchased *Jet Services V*, a Gilles Ollier designed catamaran that then held the transatlantic record of 6 days, 13 hours, 3 minutes, and renamed it *Commodore Explorer* for his sponsors, Commodore Computers. With the summer in the Southern hemisphere already in full swing it was time for the three boats to leave the cold northern hemisphere and head south. It was important that they reach the treacherous waters of the Southern Ocean during the summer months. It would be a hard enough passage when the weather was reasonable; leave it too late and the boats would have to contend with the fall when gales became more frequent, the days shorter and the weather much colder. De Kersauson was the first to leave, with *ENZA* and *Commodore Explorer* both leaving on the same day a week later. Peyron, Blake and Knox-Johnston had agreed to stage an informal race around the world to make it more exciting for those on land who would be following progress. It was a cold, blustery day when they set sail, and with the three boats having departed France, bound for France, what had started as an idea years earlier by Yves Le Cornec, had finally turned into a reality. The Trophée Jules Verne was now officially under way.

For the record since the Trophée was established, nine teams have ventured onto the course (including six failed attempts) and the record has only been broken twice:

Abandoned: 1993 – Olivier de Kersauson's tri *Charal* (damage to hull south of Cape Town SA)

Abandoned: 1993 – Peter Blake and Robin Knox-Johnston's cat *ENZA* (hole in hull after hitting submerged object in the Indian Ocean)

Record: 1993 20 April Bruno Peyron's cat *Commodore Explorer* (time: 79 days, 06 hours, 15 minutes, 56 seconds) average speed 11.35 knots

Abandoned: 1994 – Olivier de Kersauson' tri *Lyonnaise des Eaux* (actually completed the course but the time had expired)

Record:1994 1 April Peter Blake and Robin Knox-Johnston *ENZA* (time: 74 days, 22 hours, 17 minutes, 22 seconds) average speed 12 kts

Abandoned: 1996 – Olivier de Kersauson Sport Elec'-ex *Charal* (decided to leave the course after falling too far behind record)

Record: 1997 19 May Olivier de Kersauson with the tri *SPORT-ELEC* (the same boat that was *Charal* and *Lyonnaise des Eaux*. Time: 71 days, 14 hours, 22 minutes, 08 seconds)

Abandoned: 1998 – Tracy Edwards cat *Royal and SunAlliance* (this boat was ex-*ENZA* with an all-female team; they dismasted in the most remote part of the Southern Ocean between New Zealand and Cape Horn)

But that's history and pages turn.

From left to right: Jean-Baptiste Epron, Benoit Briand, Philippe Péché, Nick Moloney, Gilles Chiorri, Ronan le Goff, Bruno Peyron, Vladimir Dzalba-Lyndis, Yves le Blévec, Florent Chastel, Sébastien Josse, Yann Eliès, Hervé Jan

The Crew

The *Orange* crew

Skipper–Bruno Peyron: He is 'the Man'. Bruno is a dreamer but doesn't waste any time, he acts on his dreams and visions with passion and incredible determination. Bruno Peyron is the first name on the Jules Verne Trophy. He led the way and proved to the world that a voyage around the world under sail in under 80 days is possible. Bruno dreamed up an event, a race around the world for colossal multihulls which became known as 'The Race' and on New Year's Eve 2000–2001 six maxi-cats left Barcelona and at the stroke of midnight they were rolling over a moderate Mediterranean seaway into a new year. I was one of those sailors at sea that night, a part of Bruno's dream and creation, a part of The Race with a new breed of ocean-going racing yachts.

Throughout this Jules Verne attempt, Bruno was juggling business matters, adverse weather, 12 crew, and the unknowns of the goal. Being skipper meant many hours below deck at one of the three onboard computers; coming on deck during marginal situations and taking control; making decisions as to our next move and standing by his decisions with total belief and confidence. He brought everything to this project; his skills put him on a pedestal way above others I have sailed with, yet Bruno really showed me what it means to be a skipper.

Often Bruno would escape the computer and wander around the deck, checking everything from trim, to structure, to the crew's mental and physical wellbeing. Once satisfied he could be found sitting in the A-frame of the striker staring out to sea. Bruno has adventure and the ocean in his eyes, and the facial expressions of a proud and appreciative man. I hope he understands how grateful I am to him for the opportunities he has given me and the lessons I have learned from him.

Hervé Jan: Hervé got me the ride. We had recently been part of the team that won the final stage of the EDS Atlantic challenge on board *Kingfisher*. Hervé Jan is an unsung hero. He is a veteran of all the greatest, crewed, offshore sailing events and a winner of most: Jules Verne recordholder with Sport Elec; winner of The Race on Club Med, to name a few. Out of pure respect for Hervé I won't go on about his achievements as I know how humble he is, and he prefers to stay that way – also the book would be twice as long! What is in the past is old news as far as he is concerned. He is a genuine seafarer, a true *marin*. Hervé does not often show his romance with the sea, but he has it! He

▲ Bruno Peyron

appears to be a real hard ass – which he is, but if one of the crew was ever down he would take them under his wing and lift them. This man is one of my best friends.

Gilles Chiorri: Gilles is a real character: he took control of the refit of *Orange*, acting as skipper when the boat was dockside. Gilles juggled the job of navigator with the responsibilities of watch captain. He has a great sense of humour, and always found a great balance between fun and seri-ousness; a real prankster yet very professional, extremely talented and patient. Bruno's right-hand man.

Philippe Péché (Pépêche): Pépêche brought the essence of modern per-formance offshore multihull racing to the team. A sailing guru who has been the backbone of campaigns such as Alain Gautier's success-ful Foncia 60-foot tri campaign, and Team Adventure for The Race. In Bruno's words, 'Pépêche is always looking for something to make life faster and better. A little bit of trim here and there makes all the differ-ence.' Pépêche is also an Australian resident. He married a Perth girl during his term down under for the 1987 America's Cup in Fremantle.

Sébastien Josse (Jo Jo): Jo Jo was the Young Gun and an extremely talented sailor. He joined *Orange* after achieving a magnificent second place overall during the 2001 season in the Solitaire du Figaro – the most intense short offshore series for solo sailors. Jo Jo was our engi-neer but he is good at everything: he is a particularly good, smooth helmsman and quite a character – he and Vlad are largely responsible for my large collection of French swear words.

Yann Eliès: Yanno is another champion Figarist. Yann had also started The Race onboard Team Adventure though he had to leave the boat in New Zealand with a back injury. This voyage was therefore 'unfinished business' for both of us after our first attempts to sail around the world at full chat, fell flat. Yann has incredible helming skills and was respon-sible for our sail inventory. Yann embarked on this journey leaving behind a new wife and his second child in the making.

Vladimir Dzalba-Lyndis: Vlad is a brother surfer, born to the beach. He has an interesting past, a little James Bond like. I think, prior to *Orange*, he worked for the French equivalent of the Secret Service. Vlad's knowledge of the ocean, and waves in particular, made him a great helmsman, especially in the south where the position of the boat is absolutely vital. Vlad is one of those guys that you can really count on. He is always there to support, whether it's to keep you entertained whilst you cook at the helm under a tropical midday sun, or wrestling the jib down in the middle of the night under sheets of ice cold spray. He's real free spirit.

Jean-Baptiste Epron (J-B): J-B is firstly a sailor and secondly a cameraman. One of his tasks was to record and send back images of our journey around the world from onboard via satellite. This commitment took a great deal of time but J-B happily worked tirelessly to achieve the quality of the still and moving images that he captured at sea. It was when J-B spoke that I really wished I could better understand the French language as he always had the crew laughing.

Ronan le Goff: Ronnie was always either inside or outside the mast 38 metres or so above the deck, fixing or checking something. He is a dedicated jack-of-all-trades – the type of guy that you could recommend highly for any job, anywhere, at any time. Ronnie is into everything, a real lover of the ocean and the world. He has travelled all over and has very firm views on how to live life. When he retires from his thrill-seeking livelihood, I imagine Ronnie will park himself under a palm tree.

Yves le Blévec: Monsieur Bricolage (Mister Fix-It), Yves was our onboard boatbuilder and was kept busy fixing everything that went wrong onboard – he worked tirelessly through out the trip, literally keeping the boat afloat. Yves joined the team fresh from a very successful Mini Transat campaign. The thing I remember most clearly about Yves is his laugh.

Benoit Briand (B-B): Another master of sails, B-B is a gentle giant. There is a saying at sea aimed at those with mood swings 'knock off the peaks and fill in the valleys'. B-B is the king of this, he is patience itself, very level emotionally and always appears happy. B-B and I had competed against each other in the America's Cup, and at match racing events around the world, and had even been in the same room before but had never met until *Orange*. He is a real champion.

Florent Chastel: Florent was our onboard rigger responsible for the miles of rope, wire and fittings. Florent has intense application and strong work ethic. He takes his responsibilities very seriously and he was probably also the fittest and strongest of the crew. Although Florent's girlfriend of many years is an English teacher, Florent has only about five English words in his vocabulary!

It's really hard to sum up my feelings for these guys – all great, great guys – in a few lines. I hope that you get a better perspective of just how amazing they all are as you read on.

Together we constructed a watch system in order to make the most of particular conditions and to mantain maximum performance day and night. Basically we generally ran with three groups of four people making three watches. The *on* watch would be totally responsible for performance for a four-hour period. During this time that team is supported by a *stand-by* watch that assists the *on* watch team by changing sails, grinding, cooking etc. Another group of four are sleeping. After four hours on watch, that team would go off watch, allowing them to shed their wet clothes and climb into a bunk. Those getting out of their bunks would go on *stand-by* and the stand-by crew from the previous four hours goes into *on* watch mode. Due to the fact that Bruno needs to be available all the time for every watch, to make decisions and give instructions, he does not stand a regular watch.

24 hours a day, 7 days a week, this team of 13 men, committed to harnessing the elements that would propel us around the world. How hard we would be prepared to work would determine how long it would take us to complete a total circumnavigation under sail. If we were reckless, chances are we would not finish or, even worse, one or all of us could perish.

CHAPTER 1

'I am beginning to take in the enormity and extremity of our goal when, suddenly – CABOOM! – the sound of an enormous explosion punches through the dense air and into my body like a huge thunderclap.'

Under a plume of spray the bows drive in, their resistance and buoyancy displaying pure power. I look at the boat speed and we are doing 22 knots upwind. We are away. One of life's greatest and most dangerous adventures now lie ahead.

Our 33-metre catamaran, *Orange*, would now be our home and only means of survival for a journey around the world, to the most remote regions of our Earth, on the most inhospitable seas. Twelve Frenchmen, one Australian, one boat with two hulls, five oceans lay ahead. The quest is to make the fastest non-stop circumnavigation of the globe, under sail, in a craft of any shape or size. We are driven by the lure of Le Trophée Jules Verne (the Jules-Verne Trophy)!

We are all clad in full wet weather gear with strobes, personal emergency positioning devices, harnesses, lifejackets, the whole kit. Beating through the channel that separates Ile d'Ouessant from the rugged west coast of France, we leap over and drive through the confused swell. We are bound for the French sector of our start–finish line, an imaginary tape that stretches the length of the English Channel from France to England. The team is pumped and our vessel charging. As we push further into the channel at speeds over 25 knots our 25-tonne platform begins to launch. It's quite a sight – so much weight dispersed throughout a structure 33 metres long, 16.5 metres wide and 40 metres high from head to toe. This boat is a beast tearing apart the ocean with its bright orange claws. Our two bows pierce the sea, turning the deep green swells into an explosion of white water.

Low grey cloud sets the cold and wintry scene. Huge slabs of water explode around us, the wind is screaming. Communication is nearly impossible in such conditions. We remove our hoods in an attempt to catch anxious calls and commands. The ice-cold winter waters off the Brittany coast hit like continuous harsh slaps around the face; beads of water evaporate from my skin with the 30 knots of fresh northerly wind; my face is seized and aching.

We huddle together in the starboard cockpit and Bruno, our skipper, talks us through the start procedure. We stand shoulder to shoulder forming a circle. Bruno places his hand in the centre of the circle and forms a fist. One by one we throw in our right hands forming a ball of clenched fists butted together. We cheer like an American football team before breaking away to press on the sails and let our boat go.

Bruno calls for one reef in the mainsail. We turn our bows toward the indistinct horizon where the dark cloudy sky met the grey ocean with an array of irregular, scattered wave crests with the occasional gust of wind blending the sky and sea in bursts of spray.

We begin hoisting the headsail, halyards groaning with the load. Shouts in French scream past my ears, a language that I don't fully understand.

From my position behind Bruno, I ease the traveller, freeing the mainsail to our course, then head forward to help hoist the gennaker, a massive foresail that billows out from the masthead. The huge trampoline dividing the two hulls resembled a minefield. Explosions of water shoot randomly through the net blasting anyone in the way off their feet, upending them completely and forcing them to crawl back on their hands and knees, fingers locked into the netting. The two-metre length of our lifelines is all that is keeping us on board. We are stacking on the power, really stepping on the pedal.

I fight my way to the foot of the mast and begin to assess our position through the spray, wondering if we were across the start line. We work furiously to hoist the gennaker to the top of our 38-metre mast, then unfurled the sail to release all its power, to harness this storm and slingshot us on our way. Through a sequence of calls, five guys begin to pour power into the winches. Enough sail area to blanket the average house unfurls and the speed increases again. To quickly settle, we check loads and settings: with the boat's speed at over 30 knots we have begun our race.

▲ Slamming through the waves on our
  approach to the start

I begin coiling up the tail of the halyard used to hoist and retrieve the big gennaker neatly at the foot of the mast in preparation for any emergency drop. From this position in the centre of our massive craft I can really see the gravity of the conditions. The seas are steep. The faces of the waves are short and deep. The first 10 metres of our two sharp hulls were suspended in mid-air momentarily before we surged forward into the trough beyond burying the bows completely. The scene is unforgettable. I am beginning to take in the enormity and extremity of our goal when, suddenly – CABOOM! – the sound of an enormous explosion punches through the dense air and into my body like a huge thunderclap. I crouch down quickly and throw both arms over my head in a pointless attempt to protect myself from the 1.8-tonne mast and all the rigging crashing down around me.

I know immediately that the noise has come from the mast from the sound alone. I look skyward and catch a glimpse of the top of the rig buckling, a cloud of carbon dust blowing away in the gale then black debris, splinters of carbon, pouring from the core of the mast at its base,

▲ Preparing to start

▶ Caboom!

▲ The rigging torn through the mast wall

▶ Florent aloft

Photo: © Jean-Baptiste Epron

inches from where I am standing. I don't move. Shocked, I just look around. Two crew members appear from under the boom, crouched low as though running under the blades of a helicopter, everyone's faces shocked, stressed and frightened. My heart is trying to burst through my throat with every rapid beat. With my mouth wide open I struggle to breathe. I begin running towards the relative safety of the cockpit.

Falling into the cockpit amongst the rest of the crew, there is deep confusion, concern and disappointment. I turn again to reassess the mess. The mainsail is buckled, wrapped around the remains of the stays. The huge gennaker has lost all its majesty and is flapping uselessly. Our once powerful package for hauling us south is now a trashed mess.

We have somehow screwed up. How had this happened? We were under control, we were in command, but we have failed. We are supposed to be embarking on a voyage around the world in search of the greatest and most difficult sailing speed record and after 25 minutes our quest is over. Dismay, I guess, is the best summary. Total dismay.

Bruno's partner and the camera crew are hovering above in a helicopter. Moments before they had been beaming down at us from the open side of the chopper with fists expressing strength, thumbs up for approval, blowing kisses from their palms for luck and wellbeing. They had heard the bang and originally thought it had something to do with the integrity of the helicopter. Now shocked and sad faces mirrored ours as we signalled to the sky that everyone onboard was safe. Fuel restrictions force them to muster a wave and they peel away, the rotors clacking through the strong wind as they head back to land.

In a burst of rapid French, a plan is put forward. The first objective is to retrieve the gennaker. Getting it back on deck to stop it trailing in the sea is not going to be easy. Florent gears up to climb the stricken tube. The big problem is that all the masthead rigging has torn several metres down the mast wall, jamming both the gennaker and the mainsail. The plan is to use a line from lower on the mast, attach it to the sail, cut the original halyard and control the descent of the sails with the new line.

We gather on the forward trampoline to retrieve the mass of cloth. Before Florent has the chance to attach the second halyard, the gennaker halyard breaks and the massive sail tumbles onto the trampoline, exactly where J-B had been standing only seconds earlier. We all dive onto the sail to stop it blowing into the sea, desperately gathering it into a ball. If it washes overboard and goes under the hulls it could break off both rudders, leaving us unable to steer.

The process of getting Florent aloft and completing the preparation for the drop has taken a very long time and we are now quite well out into the Bay of Biscay. We opt to simply cut the mainsail halyard, letting the sail crash down heavily.

With sails, and more importantly Florent, down and packed away, we set a small headsail and a course for Vannes, France, the birthplace of our boat. Bruno has been busy on the phone and has a plan. We will head for the Multiplast yard that had designed, engineered and built both the boat and the mast. There we will remove the mast, assess the damage and consider our fate. We feel as though the odds are against us though; the damage is extensive.

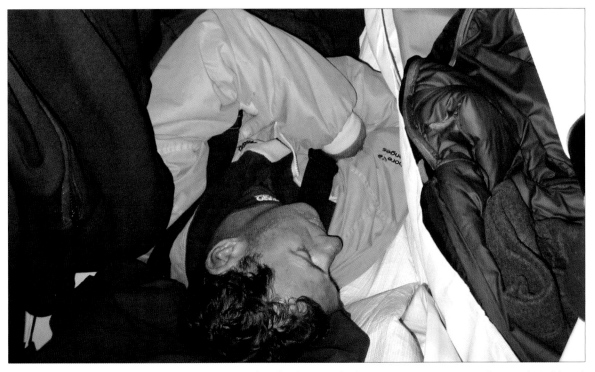

Heading back towards the Brittany coast, I am exhausted. Cold and wet, I find myself a small space on the floor of the port hull and reflect on my life, my achievements and my failures. I think about the person I have become, and how success and setback have affected my personality in the past. I am afraid for myself.

The day had begun unlike any other in my life; I had new emotions and feelings about climbing out of a dry, warm bed, feeling the warm carpet under my feet, switching on the television in search of some world news. Plentiful water streamed from the shower rose, not too hot, not too cold, but just right. I knew that these were likely to be the last, simple, too often taken-for-granted luxuries I could expect to experience for around 70 days.

The boat call came at 0500 on a dark winter morning in the historic city of Brest on the Atlantic west coast of France. Flavie, my girlfriend, and I drove from the hotel to the dock. We exchanged words desperately without much focus on what I was about to attempt to do.

▲ Totally exhausted

Photo: © Jean-Baptiste Epron

▶ What a mess

Just words, taking in the sound of her voice. I was consciously trying to have 70 days of conversation during a 15-minute drive. I knew that I would miss her and contact with many others, but how much I would miss them I didn't really appreciate.

Though my mind and soul had danced across the oceans since I was five years old, I had never before made such a commitment. This was it. I was to join a team, sail over the horizon in a southerly direction and reappear over two months later from that same horizon, heading in the opposite direction having circumnavigated the globe, with luck in good health, with all of my crewmates and a vessel still proud and powerful.

Our headlights illuminated the grey dockyard sheds. A few fishermen were unloading their catch in the now driving rain. Through the darkness the bright orange machine burst into view decorated in the distinct logo of our sponsors. She was gleaming. Lit by powerful spotlights, she looked so proud, so ready, so cool – mean and strong. Her 38-metre mast was an enormous carbon fibre wing spearing the sky. It could be seen over the rooftops from all over town, the main cross beams like strong, broad shoulders.

A crowd of onlookers appeared: representatives of various media, avid sailing enthusiasts and famous sailors. Most of the population of Brest was also standing by to wish us well on our voyage. Goodbyes always seem to take too long but as dawn broke we prepared to abandon ties with terra firma and take up a life a lot closer to nature. We prepared for an extreme dive into the unknown.

On leaving the harbour we were reminded that this attempt at the record would not only be a race against time but also against another yacht. We motored past the long and slender grey hulls of the maxi trimaran *Geronimo*, skippered by Olivier de Kersauson. The team were busily working on replacing their mast after the top section had broken away a few months earlier during training. They raised their heads momentarily and we exchanged respectful waves before continuing on our way. They planned to depart the following day.

▸ Emotional good byes... what will become of these boys?

'I had many thoughts that evening but the predominant conclusion was "failure". I think we all felt that this project was over but Bruno was the spark that continued to try to keep the flame alight.'

I woke several times during the evening as we made our way towards Quiberon and the Multiplast yard. The night sky cleared revealing perfect, crisp stars and the wind pumped strongly and consistently. We couldn't help but dwell on the fact that we could be missing the golden departure window.

Once inside the bay we still had to negotiate the Golfe du Morbihan to reach Multiplast. Bruno decided to wait until daylight to make our way through the narrow channels that separate the many islands of the Morbihan. We dropped our headsail and without any sails up at all we spent the evening sailing around the entrance at about 10 knots under the drive and power of our broken wing mast alone.

It must have been one of the coldest nights of the year. With clear skies and the northerly wind blowing at up to 40 knots, we felt as if we were hove to off Iceland. One crew member was sent out to steer for about an hour whilst another waited by the companionway hatch to assist the helmsman.

I had many thoughts that evening but the predominant conclusion was 'failure'. I think we all felt that this project was over but Bruno was the spark that continued to try to keep the flame alight. He had originally negotiated with the Orange corporation and inspired them to believe in his dream; he had developed a very strong personal and business relationship with our sponsors. We all felt that the strength of this relationship and the strength of his belief in the dream was about to be dragged over hot coals. For our part, we could not help but feel sorry that an awful lot of time, effort and money had already been laid out for our quest for a 74-day record and that we had bombed out after 25 or so minutes.

We were worried that even if Orange did decide to continue their support and bring this project back on track, we did not know if the mast could be repaired in time to get us south in time to beat the worst of the storms in the Southern Ocean. We had to leave France by 10 March at the absolute latest and this was now just 23 days away.

At sunrise we began our journey through the beautiful and picturesque Golfe du Morbihan, under the guidance of a zodiac rib. I felt as if we were being wheeled into an x-ray unit – would the verdict be all clear and positive? Or would we be out of action for a long, long time?

On our arrival at Multiplast I was surprised by how many people had arrived to see the state of our project. Many of those following our quest were in shock and wanted to see the damage to believe that this had really happened. The three most important elements along the sea wall were in place: Gilles Ollier and his design team, the creators of our machine; a large crane to remove the broken mast from the boat for proper assessment; and a team of eager boatbuilders, ready to do everything in their power to get us fixed and back on our way.

▸ A passage through the Golfe du Morbihan toward the shipyard for repairs

The wind was still howling at over 30 knots. We were beating ourselves up with comments on the wind strength and direction and how we should be charging towards the Equator in this fantastic system, but in reality the strong wind was hampering the removal of the mast. This was really frustrating. The Jules Verne is a race against time at sea but in this case there was also a race against time ashore and for us the time limit was about to expire. We needed to get on with it – now.

In order to give Gilles and Yann Penfornis, his head designer, the opportunity to get a closer look at the extent of the damage that was over 30 metres above the deck, Ronnie attached his climbing harness to the hook of the crane and, armed with a video camera, was whirled around the break and the damaged tube filming the damage. The tape was played back on the dock for the Multiplast team to begin their diagnosis.

This was a pretty difficult way to make an assessment but it did reveal what had actually failed and caused the break. Basically the windward wall of the mast had collapsed under the pressure of the topmast stay allowing the whole top section to tear away. Gilles and Yann did express some optimism but we still needed to get the mast off the boat and into the shed to find out what could be done.

This initial optimism was encouraging but we all knew that the solution was not going to be cheap and in the event that the team at Multiplast

▲ Ronan aloft to video the damage for assessment

could provide a sufficient repair in time, we would still need a further massive commitment from our sponsors. Our fate was in the hands of our sponsors who were already on a flight from Orange head office in Paris to Vannes and would arrive in time to meet with the team for dinner that evening.

We spent the day preparing the mast for the crane lift before checking into a hotel, kitting up in our cleanest team uniform and collecting our manners for our dinner with destiny. When I arrived in my room at the hotel, Bruno's partner Catherine had been into all our rooms leaving clean clothes and a small can of sweets with a card which read: *Tenezbon. Tendrement, Catherine.*

When I walked into the resturant most of the team were already seated. It had been a long day and it showed on our faces. Our table consisted of 13 worried men dressed in black with the distinctive Orange brand logo on our chests. Our faces glowed from wind burn, our eyes were red with fatigue. During dinner our fate wasn't discussed. Bruno was chirpy and positive, making jokes with the guys, trying to perk them up. We were there for our own selfish reasons but we were also there for Bruno and his dream – a dream that had been conceived by him, that included us, and that we all really believed in.

When we left the restaurant after dessert and wearily headed back to a soft dry bed, Bruno started a long evening of discussion, explanation and planning with our corporate partners. I think I speak for all involved when I say that we were grateful not to be in his shoes.

On 16 February we all woke early and went down to the boat. The wind had dropped enough to let us lift out the mast. In the event the process was pretty quick with many helpful hands and before long we were all able to see the damage. The Multiplast team prodded, tapped and tore away damaged laminate to get an idea of the extent of the damage. Whilst we wheeled the mast into the shed, a design and construction forum gathered in Gilles's office.

Moments later Bruno disappeared. I am not sure what caused the turn around but without any hint of a verdict on our fate we all began to feel very positive. Maybe it was a good night's sleep or the realisation that *Geronimo* was on her way and we were driven to chase and beat her to the record. We met for lunch and our good vibes were confirmed by Bruno – the repair was on and he issued a press release announcing that we would have another go.

Several assessments needed to be made. We required many new custom fittings and stays. Some needed to be manufactured in the USA and would be flown over to France. The structural integrity of the whole 38-metre mast was now under question and would need ultrasonic analysis.

Everybody's focus flicked. There was a lot of work to be done. The

▲ The stress of being a campaign director as well as skipper

boat itself was ready for departure four days ago but it was now time to get ourselves prepared. I hit the gym and worked on regaining fitness lost over the preceding months and the weight lost during the long year racing *Kingfisher*.

Boats are never really ready – you can work on them continually. But I have reached a point where I can say 'OK, she's ready. Am I?' The greatest mistake I made during my preparations for another event, the 1999 Mini Transat, was that I had invested all my energies in the boat's job list. During my first night at sea in that race I felt that the boat had actually been ready for months but I wasn't ready for what was coming. I had not invested enough time in my own preparation and the bottom line was that race almost cost me my life. What I needed was a great deal of physical and mental strength and conditioning, and for me this was a chance to leave really well prepared.

The lights burned brightly 24 hours a day, 7 days a week in the aluminium boatbuilding shed where the tireless team ran their own watch system to work around the clock on the repair. It's impossible to express enough thanks to this team. These guys' and girls' lives were put on hold to turn this situation around for us – no family life, no normality. Sleep-deprived but focused, the team worked relentlessly on the repair.

The piece of mast that had broken away from the top was about 1.5 metres long and the initial idea was to rejoin the two sections by laminating them with many layers of carbon fibre. After closer analysis it was decided that due to the extent of damage caused by the halyards tearing down the mast wall it would be more efficient to make a completely new 5-metre section at the top of the mast. The original moulds for the mast were prepared and modified so that the layers of carbon fibre could be laid down. The moulds are a complete profile of the mast in two halves. The 16-foot/5-metre section would be laid up in the two half moulds and cooked at a temperature of 120° C to cure the resin. The two half shells would then be joined together. The new top and the rest of the mast would be scarfed together with sheets of carbon fibre. Once this was all together again, the paint would be applied and the fittings put back. If time became too tight we would skip the painting.

As the process continued and the clock ticked away, *Geronimo* was on course and ahead of the existing record...

Part of my fitness training was to go for a bike ride every morning for about an hour. The Morbihan is a beautiful part of Brittany and I remember thinking that these could be the last few days I spent alive on land! You may think this a melodramatic statement but the reality is that this way of life is dangerous. The risk factor is enormous and there is an element of truth involved when people exclaim 'You guys are mad!' On my way to the boat on the morning of the start of the Whitbread Round the World

Race this emotion was so strong that I wrote a letter, my own 'obituary' if you like, and gave it to my parents with instructions only to open it if something bad happened. If nothing happened they were to give it back to me at the finish. I keep it in a small chest with my stage medals and souvenirs from that race at my parents home in Australia, unopened.

Thirteen days and nights rolled by – not that those inside the shed ever noticed the difference between night and day as they worked under the bright lights. Rolling back the shed doors in the morning of Friday 1 March 2002 was like revealing a gang of coal miners emerging from deep underground after two weeks' hard toil – tired and weary, their faces black from carbon fibre dust, their eyes red, they walked wearily with aching backs.

This was the absolute earliest day that the mast could leave the shed and possibly be lifted back onto the boat. Incidentally, possibly the last potentially good weather system was in place for setting up a departure from Ushant the next day. Bruno, Gilles Chiorri (navigator), Yann Penfornis and Eric Mas (who would provide weather advice from his company Meteo Consult) announced at a press conference that day at lunchtime that we would leave the same afternoon from Vannes at about 1800, set a course for Ushant and cross the start line of the Jules Verne Trophy for the second time tomorrow morning Saturday 2 March 2002.

As fate would have it, just as Bruno was making his announcement, the

▲ Hervé and Bruno assess the damage with Yann Penfornis

▲ Bruno announces… we will leave
again today!

▶ Yann loading the mainsail

news broke that Olivier de Kersauson and his crew had abandoned their attempt after encountering problems with the steering of their giant trimaran. The tables had turned. When we left for our first departure, we had motored past them stepping their repaired mast and that day our attempt failed. Two weeks later, we were stepping our repaired mast when we received the news that they had suffered a terminal set back and were out of the chase.

Bruno's announcement obviously meant that we had to stretch our resources for the final push. The first day of March was a busy one. Through the madness and the driving rain we stepped our repaired mast and loaded our sails. I don't recall many of the crew having family or loved ones there for our second departure but I do recall a desperate run around, shaking hands with a flurry of 'mercis' to everyone who had helped once again to get us to sea. By dusk, at 1800 as Bruno had promised, we slipped away from Vannes and into the darkness.

One minute we were hectically working on preparation, the next we were off again.

▲ Hastily stowing sails and equipment
▲ Bruno gives the order and with a final wave we head back out to sea for our second chance

CHAPTER 3

'Orange was blasting across a smooth sea at 30
knots. The look of sheer delight on the
faces of my crewmates said that all was
right with our world.'

We left Vannes on the Friday evening and spent a rough night getting the boat ready for the trip. It had been a hasty departure, but Gilles Chiorri and Bruno had been studying the weather and had seen a window we could not afford to miss. It had been a big day. We had put the repaired mast back just six hours before we left. The day had been spent frantically tensioning the rigging and stowing sails in the relentless rain. Onlookers muttered that we looked far from ready, that this was madness. But we knew we had to leave, we had no choice, it was now March and this was our final chance. If we missed this weather we would have to wait until next winter for another shot. If we crossed the startline early on the Saturday morning we might have a clear run down to the tradewinds off Portugal.

We arrived at the start area in the early morning. The wind was blowing 25 to 30 knots from the northeast, forecast to strengthen during the day and gradually veering to the east. These were perfect conditions to slingshot us south, and we were ready for the trip. The northerly element made the wind cold, whipping icy spray off the grey sea. Ahead we could now see the low profile of Ile d'Ouessant and within minutes we had passed it, leaving it to port, and were able to turn the bows to face south. We crossed the start line for the second time at 0836 and 21 seconds (French time) on 2 March – the precise moment the clock started ticking. From that moment on we were in the race.

Sixteen days had passed since our first attempt, and for all of us onboard *Orange* we knew we had been given a reprieve. The mast damage could have scuttled our plans for a Jules Verne record that season, but the amazing dedication shown by the team at Multiplast had the mast repaired and back in the boat well ahead of their original three-week estimate.

We would be heading south for three weeks until we reached the cold waters of the Southern Ocean and turned the boat to the east. Our main objective from the moment we crossed the startline was to be back off Ile d'Ouessant by 2356 (French time) on 12 May which would give us the record by a whopping 31 seconds. Any less than that would be cutting it too close. Any more would be gravy.

The second departure had been a little more subdued than the first with the mast break still foremost in everyone's mind. We were confident that the repair was more than adequate and there was no need for concern, but human nature ensured a hint of caution. We were all exhausted from working long days and nights but with a new 5-metre section scarfed onto the old mast, and new rigging, the huge wing was ready for the voyage. Just to give an idea of how big the mast is and what a big job it was to repair it: it is possible to send a man to the top of the mast, up the inside!

▶ Our *Orange* claws tear into the swells

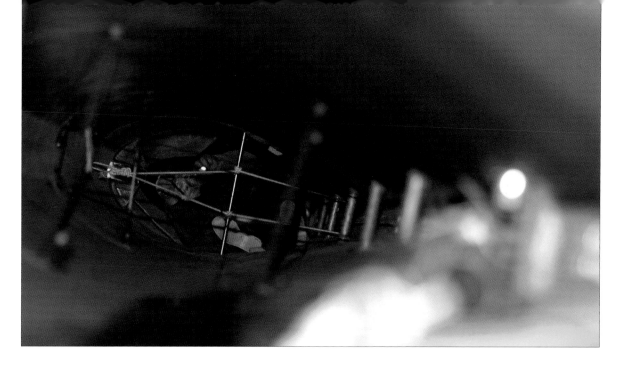

It had been just over two weeks since we first sailed past Ile d'Ouessant (Ushant as it's known in English); this time we crossed the startline with three reefs in the main and no headsail. Bruno was not taking any chances. The sea was quite rough with strong counter currents and gusty winds. We crossed the line on the starboard tack, gybed shortly there-after, and then started to pile on sail.

We gathered together once again in the port cockpit and threw one last wave to our camera crew recording history-in-the-making from a heli-copter hovering overhead. I could not help wondering when we would see them again. Would the faces of my 12 crewmates really be the only others I would see for more than two months?

First the staysail went up and the boat speed immediately jumped to over 25 knots. We then threw out a reef and set the storm spinnaker. Our plan was simple: to get progressively into the race, give everyone enough time to get into a rhythm, and then gently pile on the power. By mid-after-noon we were already building up our speed – *Orange* was blasting across a smooth sea at 30 knots. The look of sheer delight on the faces of my crewmates said that all was right with our world. We might have experi-enced a setback a few weeks earlier but we had come out of it better prepared and more ready than ever for the challenge that lay ahead.

Through this succession of sail changes came the actual realisation of the scale of our endeavour. I had found that under pressure it was diffi-cult for most my crewmates to utter a single word in English and likewise for me in French. This was obviously a very daunting and somewhat fright-ening discovery. I was part of a floating French colony. To describe the situation as total immersion would be something of an understatement.

▲ Hervé inside the mast tube

Log 1

Very difficult beginning.
Trying to decide what sails
to put up in strong winds.
Running south in strong
northerly winds. Between 2
reefs and full mainsail with
storm spinnaker.
Last night lots of shipping
approaching Cape Finisterre.
Had to flap the spinnaker to
shoot behind the path of a
super tanker at around 2300
hours. Quite stressful!
This morning whilst still
dark, the front section of
our trampoline tore open and
almost lost sail that fell
through the hole into the
sea. Now repaired and safe
again.
Getting warmer. Can feel
hands again! It's pretty wet
and cold as ever.
Boat speed 25kts, you
quickly get used to this
speed.
Currently surrounded by
lightning. Prepared to
shorten sail but happy to be
making good progress and
approaching the latitude of
Gibraltar 1000 miles/1,600
kilometres from start – not
bad for a weekend's work.
Happy to be at sea.

I thought back to our first departure: maybe I didn't know my limits; maybe I was heading for a disaster. I had no idea. It was cold and wet, and *Orange* was heaving in the confused seaway. I sat in numb silence for a moment until I remembered something J-B Epron had said to me earlier in the day, something I will remember forever. He said 'Days like today are very special. It's like when you were ten years old and you said to yourself... someday I'm going to do that!'

As we settled into the first night at sea, some of the lads were a little seasick from a combination of the motion, fatigue and anxiety. I thought about our friends on *Geronimo*. Olivier de Kersauson and his crew had found an excellent weather window and they rode a fair wind all the way to the Equator, making the trip in a little over nine days. They were off the coast of Brazil when their steering mechanism developed problems and they had a tough decision: face the Southern Ocean with a compromised steering system, or head back home and try again another day. We knew how difficult it must have been for Olivier and his crew. The memory of abandoning The Race on *Playstation* was still fresh in my mind. It was a fair warning to the rest of us; the race can be one of attrition. We needed to be vigilant and keep our boat in top condition all the way to the finish line. There was a long way to go and much could happen along the way.

See Log 1

▲ The boys are happy

Photo: © Jean-Baptiste Epron

The fact that a section of the trampoline had opened up was very concerning. The trampoline is basically strong fishing net under tension. It provided a platform that allowed the crew to move freely around the massive boat. There are three main sections that make up around 90 per cent of the working deck space. To lose any one of these three sections made for a very dangerous and difficult work environment.

By Day 2 we had passed Gibraltar sailing a narrow corridor of wind funnelling between two high-pressure systems. To our right a firm high was centred over the Azores, and to our left there was another high over southern Portugal. We were careful not to get too close to the windless zones near their edges; in order to remain in the wind required plenty of manoeuvring and sail changes. The weather was squally with 30 knots one minute and calm the next. I counted 14 sail changes in 24 hours taking us through our entire sail inventory, but despite the hard work we were glad to be moving south at a good speed. With all the rain and sail changes the boat was a damp mess below but no one cared. At the end of our watches we piled into our bunks and slept the sleep of the dead.

◀ Exhausting sail changes

▶ Overleaf... This is where we belong

CHAPTER 4

*'The hunt is on for the slightest puff of wind.
Every mile gained towards the south brings us
that much closer to deliverance.'*

Quickly we became part of miles and miles of undulating ocean, picking our way along invisible highways to the next weather system. Sailing around the world is like playing a massive game of chess with the boat and the weather systems as giant pieces. We knew that to break the record we had to finish the course, and with 13 men on board, all with their own ideas of where the 'reasonable limit' stood, it was going to be an exercise in balance and restraint. While our main objective was to break Olivier de Kersauson's overall record of 71 days 14 hours, 22 minutes and 08 seconds, we couldn't help but think about the many other records we could lay claim to along the way. The first was the fastest time to the Equator. When Peter Blake and Robin Knox-Johnston sailed that way on *ENZA* in 1994 (their second attempt), they took a remarkable 7 days, 4 hours and 11 minutes to sail from Ile d'Ouessant to latitude 0. *Geronimo* took 9 days and 7 hours to cover the same distance. Our weather conditions were nowhere near as perfect as those they had experienced, but we were making good speed and keeping a wary eye on the clock and the distance to go.

At the speed we were sailing south it did not take too long for the weather to warm up and by the middle of the third day we had hung up our Gore-Tex shells and changed into shorts and T-shirts. I was very happy to be at sea and despite the tough sailing of the first few days I knew I was exactly where I wanted to be. The crew were settling into a routine and laughter could be heard throughout the boat. Once the sun came out the mood improved even more and we made an attempt to clean up the boat and ourselves. Bruno had appointed a 'minister of the interior' and Vlad ruled with a rod of iron. He soon had our home sparkling clean but nothing on a boat remains tidy and dry for very long as Gilles Chiorri noted in his log:

We might be in warmer latitudes, but it can get quite damp from time to time. A short while back the companionway hatch was left slightly open and all of a sudden it started to resemble Niagara Falls.

By the third day we were approaching the Canary Islands and were free falling south at speed. Bruno was keen to pass outside the island group for fear of getting caught between them. Sometimes you can get a boost from riding the wind funnel between the islands but at other times you can get stuck in the lee of the higher islands and slow right down. It was too early in the trip to be rolling the dice, so Bruno opted to go around the outside and fortunately the wind played along. We put in a gybe to the west and saw no sign of land. Bruno also wanted to pass outside the Cape Verde Islands and to make some westing before we reached the Doldrums. We were already beginning to position ourselves for this area of light winds which is narrower to the west; it was important to head in that direction without going too far out of our way.

The tradewinds were unusually light and Bruno and Gilles poured over the weather charts looking for a sign of the wind changing in our favour. Bruno's email to our PR company Mer et Media read:

We're impatiently waiting for the weather files to announce a strengthening of the wind more from an easterly direction. That would enable us to pass outside of Cape Verde Islands (670 miles/1,078 kilometers away at 1300) on just one gybe.

Meanwhile we took advantage of the easy conditions to send Florent up the mast, both inside and outside, a tough job that he took in his stride. There is a halyard rigged inside the mast, which we used to hoist him aloft. He had a walkie-talkie with him so that we could communicate from below while he made the long, claustrophobic trip to the top. It was his first opportunity to take a good look at the state of the repairs. An hour later when he returned to the deck he reported that all was well. I didn't envy him the job. It's dark and stuffy in the mast, to say nothing of the motion 38 metres off the deck. I couldn't help thinking what it would be like if the mast broke and fell into the sea with someone inside it. A terrible death.

As we neared the Cape Verdes I thought about the last time I had passed here just a few months earlier. I was racing the Transat Jacques Vabre a double handed (two crew) race across the Atlantic from France to Brazil. We had had a good race up until that point but by sailing too close to the islands we lost 60 miles/96 kilometres to the opposition in one morning. It was very painful, but a lesson was learned. We had no such bad luck on *Orange* and continued cruisin' south at good speed donning foul weather gear again as the boat powered along at 30 knots making a bit too much spray. It was hot, but we were glad to be stonkin'. We were happy in the knowledge that we were ahead of where *Sport Elec* had been at the same point into the trip. At night we started to notice strong cloud formations and knew that the big squalls of the tropics were not far away.

The tradewind conditions still called for a lot of sail changes and gybes making for a busy time on board. Yann Eliès noted in his log:

Our very full set of foresails enables us to constantly adapt to the slightest variations of wind in strength and angle. This results in an impressive number of manoeuvres. Thirty-eight sail changes since the start.

Below decks Bruno was also keeping score, but in a different way:

The boys are ready for the deep south. They're manoeuvring to perfection, sleeping like babies and are devouring food like ogres. This complicated navigation has obliged us to be a hundred per cent attentive and responsive. So far, we haven't been able to complain about a single false manoeuvre.

◄ An idea of proportion... Florent is 5'11" or 180cm; working aloft is physically demanding and dangerous

We had taken onboard over one tonne of food and sundry items such as cleaning products toilet paper, ketchup etc, separated by what was required weekly and vacuum bagged into weekly packages. These were stored in the hollow back beam and brought forward into the cooking area only when required. It's strange to think that we really suffered from a lack of space on a boat so large. Our food was mostly dehydrated and very similar to the meals prepared for astronauts who travel into space. Many cringe at the description of our diet but the meals are actually quite good. Hey, I am on tour with a bunch of Frenchies, they are very serious about food. To rehydrate our meals all we had to do was simply add hot water and a few minutes later, *voila*, a meal fit for a French man. We even took two rather large legs of salted, smoked ham that can last up to two months on a boat and six months if it were stored in a dry climate. Don't forget the cheese; we took a few big chunks of cheese but these luxuries really did make a difference to life and attitude onboard.

While the trades were difficult and demanding, the first major obstacle we faced was to be the Doldrums. We were going to encounter them long before we got to the Equator and if we were going to set a new record to the Equator we would have to navigate through this area of light winds very carefully. Our position to the west, that Bruno and Gilles had so carefully planned, would definitely help our boat speed, but nothing was guaranteed. The French have their own name for the Doldrums: the Pot au Noir which literally translated is Black Pot. No one really knows why. Some say that the sailors of old gave it the name because of its huge

▲ A quick gennaker change

▶ More sail changes

Log 2

Not far from the Equator now. Very hot today. Hoping that there are not too many squalls about tonight. Night skies have been clear and full of stars. Tonight we plan to work out how to use a planetarium that Vlad has smuggled onboard.

Last night we had a reminder of just how loaded the boat is and how easily this trip could be all over in a second. We were cruising along in 15 knots of wind doing 20 knots boat speed when a loud bang broke the peaceful night air. The swivel on the top of the gennaker had exploded. Alarmingly it made a very similar sound to the mast failing. First thoughts were that a turning block had torn down the mast, which would mean that no large downwind sails could be used for the rest of the voyage. Fortunately the situation was less dramatic and within an hour the sail was back up and we were charging south again. Learnt some new French phrases during this episode!

▶ Sébastien and Vladimir and that damned swivel that failed the previous evening

storms with clouds as black as night. Other, less poetic, sources claim that it was the slave traders running between Africa and the West Indies that called it the Pot au Noir because the bodies of slaves who died of thirst aboard becalmed ships were thrown overboard. There is probably a grain of truth in both stories with the Pot au Noir being famous for its calms as well as its dark and violent storms.

There is a reason for the area having such a volatile climate. The Doldrums occur where the great air masses from the northern hemisphere and southern hemisphere meet. It is also an area of tremendous heat being so close to the Equator and the ocean is subject to day after day of relentless, pounding sunshine. The result is hot, moist, electrically charged air that can give rise to enormous storms. One moment the ocean is glassy calm, the next it is whipped up by 40 knots of moisture-laden wind. It makes for difficult sailing as the sail changes are endless, to say nothing of the stifling conditions below decks.

Once in the Doldrums we began the slow crawl towards latitude 0, the Equator. When you are racing a fleet in these waters you know that everyone is generally slowing but for us the clock keeps ticking and seconds are still seconds, minutes still minutes. It's frustrating and concerning because you never know how long the calm will last... it could be hours or even days. The day before our Equator crossing I wrote in my logbook.

 See Log 2

Eighty miles/128 kilometres north of the Equator we slowed to a stop. The ocean turned glassy and the swells looked like they were covered in a thin layer of oil. Any chance of breaking *ENZA's* record was quietly dismissed. We just hoped to keep the damage to a minimum and searched for every puff of wind. The sun beat down turning the cabin into a hellhole. Above decks was not much better even though we all crouched in the shade of the mainsail. In the middle of the day, with the sun directly overhead, the shade was minimal, so we dipped buckets into the ocean and doused ourselves with seawater. Helming required every bit of concentration we could muster which was particularly difficult as there was no shade at all back aft. The helmsman had to stand with his feet in two buckets of water to keep cool. Gilles summed up the mood on board:

The hunt is on for the slightest puff of wind. Every mile gained towards the south brings us that much closer to deliverance.

Log 3

Welcome back to the
Doldrums. Very, very typical
conditions... stinking hot
with light, shifty winds. We
have just begun a succession
of tacks. We are slow, the
big girl is struggling to
drag herself through the
sea. Our average is probably
two knots of boat speed.

The deliverance he was referring to was the tradewind belt south of the Equator. Once we broke through the calms we could count on good wind all the way into the Southern Ocean. My log was not much different. In addition to the trying conditions I was also dealing with some personal issues. I had fallen off my mountain bike a few days before the start and the wound on my left leg had become infected. The problem was that the wound was at exactly the same height as the sheets crossing the trampoline, so I kept knocking off the scab. I had been trying to ignore the problem but decided to pay a visit to the doc to get some treatment. I thought it wise to get this sorted before pulling my boots back on for the next month.

 See Log 3

The slow progress allowed Vlad to dive and check the hull and appendages below the water. In an email to Mer et Media he wrote:

The watchword onboard remains unchanged. Whether in a blow or dead calm, we have to keep a particularly careful eye on the boat's condition and on the level of wear and tear on equipment. Today is the first day that Orange has been sailing really slowly. I've made the most of it to dive and inspect the condition of the hulls and appendages. Not the slightest scratch to report.

Later that night we saw a huge lightning storm to the west. It was a massive show of electrically charged air. Giant thunderheads formed above us bringing a light but steady breeze and the following morning at precisely 0736 GMT we crossed the Equator. It had taken us 7 days and 22 hours to make the trip from Ile d'Ouessant. Peter Blake, Robin Knox-Johnston and the crew of *ENZA* had shown us that records were there to be broken but it's never a given. For now it remained theirs. We were free of the Pot au Noir and into fresh southeasterlies.

▶ Crossing the Equator

▶ Classic doldrums

Photo: © Jean-Baptiste Epron

▶ Overleaf... I love this boat!

CHAPTER 5

*'The high is getting bigger and bigger all the time
and is closing the door to the east.'*

Log 4

Having a bit of computer trouble at the moment. The obvious news of yesterday was that we crossed the equator and are now in the southern hemisphere. Managed to sleep through another one, this being my sixth crossing under sail. Neptune appeared in the morning and we all got a present from our shore team. No points for guessing that my present was a French phrase book. It was a real treat, bit of a laugh.

Yesterday afternoon the breeze just kept slowly building and by evening 20-25 knots upwind. Quite lumpy! Boat speed around 20-22 knots could go faster but don't want to stress the boat as she's still heavy with food, etc.

Temperature isn't really dropping but we are forced to wear full wet weather gear as it's so wet on deck. So, it's hot, sticky and very wet. No complaints though, as we are heading south at speed.

▶ Holding her back to 22 knots of boat speed in order to suppress the slamming

The first real milestone of our trip was now behind us and we were into the southern hemisphere. For the next seven weeks we would be 'down under' as they say, and I was already looking up at the night sky searching for the Southern Cross. I woke up in the morning to see Neptune come on board to do some initiations. Actually I thought I recognised a bit of Gilles Chiorri in Neptune, but couldn't be sure. He was there to pay a visit to Ronan, Florent, Benoit and Sébastien who had just crossed the equator by boat for the first time. Sébastien later wrote down his feelings about the crossing:

This was the first time that I had crossed the Doldrums and it was a bit like what I'd seen on the television. I've seen all the videos of the big races and have been through the same thing in terms of atmosphere. It was damp, rather warm with a threatening sky and big squalls. However, we did not go through any squalls and only had a couple of spots of rain.

 ## See Log 4

It was now time to focus on the next big obstacle that lay in our path – our attention turned to the South Atlantic High. Both hemispheres have their large areas of high pressure, but the one in the South Atlantic is particularly dominant. It is also totally unforgiving if you try and cut the corner off it. There were two ways to deal with the High. We could either sail the more direct route to the east and face headwinds until we neared the latitude of Cape Town, or we could sail the much longer western route leaving the High to port and enjoy winds at first from the southeast. They would slowly move into the east and then the north as we sailed further south. Bruno and Gilles were keeping their options open as Bruno discussed in a chat session with Mer et Media:

It's a little too early to say what we're going to do but we're sure that in a couple of days from now we will have to make a decision. Whatever we opt for, we'll have to choose between going west round the High along the Brazilian coast, or cutting straight across it, even if it means beating into the wind. The High is getting bigger and bigger all the time and is closing the door to the east.

While Bruno and Gilles discussed their options, the rest of us still had to keep the boat moving as fast as possible. It was still brutally hot on deck but at least we had wind and were making good speed. In fact we were stonkin' along at 25 to 27 knots under full main and solent. We were still

Log 5

Woken this morning by the
mainsheet block pad-eye
breaking. Flew out of my
bunk but situation now
rectified by drilling into
main beam and lashing the
turning block back in place.
Now trying to change out all
of the similar high load
attachment points by lashing
through the bolt holes
direct to the structure with
aramid rope. Have a few big
squalls about and are a
little overpowered with one
reef and staysail.

dodging squalls that left a confused seaway. The wind started to drop off at around 0100 on 12 March (Day 11) and left a rather confused sea between squalls. It might have been the mainsail slatting between squalls, but no matter what it was, I woke up around dawn to another loud bang.

 *See Log 5*

The South Atlantic High had been looking as though it was increasing in size, threatening to block our route south, but upon further investigation Gilles had better news for us:

The situation is not as bad as we thought yesterday. Yesterday, the High literally barred the way to the Deep South, but today we can see that it is leaving a small door open to the east and one to the west.

Since maxi-catamarans are not good at sailing into the wind in light airs it would be better to skirt round to the west and to gybe a number of times. The decision was made and we steered a course slightly west of south. It was an easy decision to agree with. For now we were almost 1,000 miles/1,600 kilometres ahead of where *Sport Elec* had been at the same time and there was no need for bold, aggressive moves. With the wind at 90° to our course, we eased sail and started to knock off the miles.

A good navigator is always looking beyond the immediate to the weather that might be expected in a few days time. By any measure Bruno and Gilles were a formidable team and I was sure that they would guide us south without finding any parking lots, something that would not be easy since the High has a mind of its own and could easily slide to the west and block our way. While we were keeping a wary eye on the barometer, Gilles and Bruno were watching a small low that had developed to the south of the High. Bruno was hoping we could hook onto the northern edge of the low and ride it south. If we got it right we could get 15 to 20 knots of wind on the beam that would propel us into the Southern Ocean. First though we had to run the tightrope between less wind to the east and a shorter distance to sail, or more wind to the west and further to sail. Even with the sophisticated weather equipment we had on board it would not be easy. In fact our best instrument was one that had been around for centuries: the barometer had helped to guide the old sailing ships across the oceans and would be invaluable to us. We planned to latch onto an isobar that gave us good winds and stick with it. If the barometer rose at all we would turn away from the centre of the High, and if it dropped we knew we should turn left and cut our distance. We needed a good 48 hours to skirt the edge taking into account some an inevitable drop in speed.

See Log 6

Log 6

While the big picture involved dodging weather patterns and keeping the boat moving fast, day-to-day life brought its minor problems. Soon after we crossed the equator the toilet in the port hull stopped working. We had been given some Ecover biodegradable bags. (Ecover was the sponsor of one of my competitors in the Open 60 Class, Mike Golding, who had also set a sailing record around the world but in a mono-hull and in the opposite direction, east–west against the prevailing winds and currents. Ecover makes environmentally friendly household goods.) We rigged up a simple toilet using the bags and a bucket.

The guys were also getting into some lighthearted antics – they were shaving their beards into stupid shapes and Pépêche was winning the competition by a mile with massive sideburns and a moustache. One night I ran across the trampoline to the windward hull and stood by Hervé on the helm trying to familiarise myself with the set up and sail trim when I noticed a pair of fake breasts staring back at me from the martingale. The martingale is a frame arrangement at the front of the boat which basically stops the boat from breaking in half with the mast loading. It took a short while for my eyes to focus on what I was seeing, and the boys, watching for my reaction, broke into hysterics when they saw my face. The mood on board was still great with everyone getting along just fine. The guys were quite happy with my collection of French swear words, but I had a growing concern that I had missed something in my understanding of the trip. I wrote in my log:

```
We are now over 18° S and
still in shorts and T-s,
bathing in the spray off our
hulls or with buckets
several times a day. The
days still pack some strong
squalls but the general wind
keeps the boat speed around
20 knots. At around midnight
the air cools a little and
the clouds disappear leaving
beautiful clear starry
nights. This is definitely
the greatest place in the
world for night sailing.
Shorts, bare feet, no shirt
to protect you from the sun,
no hat, no sun glasses...
awesome!
```

See Log 7

Log 7

The most common phrase used on board was ironically an English one: 'so far so good'. It summed up the trip perfectly.

As we continued south life on board settled into a familiar rhythm. Gilles and Bruno spent much of their day discussing strategy. The rest of us took our turns at the helm and trimming sails while *Orange* just ate up the miles. A small bubble of high pressure developed just ahead of us and we had to steer even more to the west. We would be losing distance on *Sport Elec* but there was very little we could do about it. We had more than 1,600 miles/2,575 kilometres in hand over *Sport Elec* which sounds like a lot but there was a long way to go and anything could happen. Then all of a sudden we ran out of wind. I was sitting down below writing up a report for the website when I noticed that there was no sound of water flowing past the hull. It was eerily quiet. There is a sense of frustration in my log:

```
We are so far west right now
I fear that I may have
accidentally signed up for
an east-west tour around the
world - whoops!
```

▸ Overleaf... Sometimes frustrating but always beautiful

Log 8

Well this has been the first time that we have actually STOPPED! I am though glad to be feeling the full influence of the High because I know that there is wind beyond it. I'm just a bit impatient to get through to the other side and begin heading EAST!

Not sure how far ahead of Sport Elec but believe its around 1600 miles. If so we will watch some of that diminish over the next 36 hours until we find a new stream of breeze.

The temperature is great. A bit hot during the days and beautiful at night. Before long it will be freezing our butts off and we know it so everyone has stopped complaining about the heat. Didn't sleep last off watch. Lay around listening to music a tad concerned about rate of progress. Did I mention that I am looking forward to heading EAST! Never have I been this far west in a passage out of the Atlantic. Its killing me to think that a course with its only marks being the Southern Capes and our next being Cape of Good Hope and we are on the opposite side of the Atlantic, still sailing AWAY from South Africa! Guess I need to just take the good with the bad – just frustrated. We have had a pretty good run so far. Tonight will be another tough one but with a mirror sea, clear skies, you can be sure that it will be spectacular.

All right! As I am sitting here writing we have started to move at around 7 knots of boat speed. The sound of water past the hull is bliss.

Keep going girl!

See Log 8

During the night we gybed twice. Slowly the new wind picked up to 10 knots and remained there, and then it slowly started to build – 12 knots steady, then 15. We sheeted in the big gennaker and *Orange* gathered speed. With each mile south the temperature dropped and for the first time since entering the tropics we were able to sleep better at night. The days were still warm but the nights were cool. To add to the fun we were able to steer a course east of south for a period. Gilles said:

We are on the slip road to the motorway. The motorway is there but we know there will be some more roadworks to slow us down before the great disturbed flows of the south.

The roadworks he was referring to was another ridge of high pressure that was developing to the south of us. It reached all the way to the coast of Argentina not allowing any way to get past. We would have to sail straight through the light winds at the centre of the high, slowing us down before we found the westerlies down south. Just now we were sailing along at 18 to 20 knots. The sailing was not a problem for the crew, just

a bit wet, but the close reaching conditions were hard on the boat. *Orange* slammed into each wave and, at 20 knots, the slamming was severe. We had a lot of supplies and fuel on board and the boat was heavy. We couldn't afford any breakages, so it was important to baby it a little.

All the westing we had made to get around the high had us 550 miles/885 kilometres to the west of *Sport Elec's* 1997 track. Once we got through the next area of high pressure we would be able to set a course for a point south of Cape Town. We were all keen to leave the South Atlantic behind and get into the real meat of the voyage: the transit of the Southern Ocean. Gilles distributed mittens to all the crew in anticipation of the cold seas to the south, and wrote in his log:

The sea is still tropical blue and the sunshine strong. We altered course to the southeast this morning, which is synonymous with leaving the high behind. The boat is in great shape and we are continuing to discover and fine tune our settings.

▲ Continual attention to detail

◀ Sleeping quarters; basic but perfect for recharging the batteries

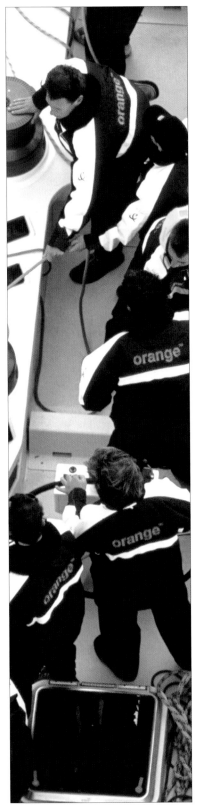

As we slipped south we started to encounter more sea life. One afternoon we passed the carcass of a dead whale and an hour later surfed past two live ones. We were heading towards Tristan da Cunha, a small group of islands on the edge of the Southern Ocean named after the Portuguese sailor who first discovered them in 1713. The islands were abandoned in 1961 after a volcanic eruption but they have since been repopulated and now serve as a military and meteorological station for the British Defence Force. Apparently it's a paradise for giant prawns but we couldn't stop to check them out.

It was our custom at each watch change to slow down a little so that we could carry out a complete inspection of the boat without getting washed over the side. It was a pitch-dark night and Philippe was carrying out the inspection. He was on the trampoline when he suddenly caught a glint of something in his headlamp. He bent down and picked up an oblong pin about 20 inches/50 centimetres long. Instinctively he looked aloft at the headboard for the mainsail certain that the pin was from the headboard carriage. Moments later Florent was hoisted aloft and he returned to deck with the news that indeed the end cap had broken off the custom headboard carriage and one of the rods was missing. We immediately dropped the mainsail and got to work. Florent went back aloft to clean up the damaged track while Yves and Ronan set about repairing the headboard car. Working under the light of their headlamps they made some new carbon endplates and we were back in business by early morning. The main was rehoisted to the first reef, the gennaker sheeted in and *Orange* was off once again at 20 knots. Had Philippe not noticed the pin on the tramp we could have really damaged the track. Bruno summed up the situation:

The incredible responsiveness of the crew never ceases to amaze me. The breakage had hardly been announced before there were nine on deck to slow the boat, send a man up the mast, bring down the main and carry out the repair. We knew that the Jules Verne would be demanding technically and complicated meteorologically, more than ever we realize that it is a story about people.

As predicted we started to slow down again as we ran into the area of high pressure. There was nothing we could do to avoid it and somehow the knowledge that there was no way around made it easier to deal with. The barometer started to rise and we shook the reef out of the main. The wind kept backing until it was right on the nose again and *Orange* went back into slamming upwind mode. The bottom batten in the mainsail broke and we had to drop the sail, sort the batten and rehoist, a task we were getting quite good at since it was not the first time the batten had broken. Bruno wrote in his log:

We're going to have to suffer the passage of the anticyclone today. As soon as the wind and sea offer us a good angle of attack we will be descending further south. The temperature of the water and air has cooled off and we are about to start another rhythm of life with the speed, the cold and the discomfort of a boat that will be surfing sometimes rather brutally on the ocean.

A few hours later we crossed latitude 40° S and entered the infamous Southern Ocean. A great wandering albatross cruised by in welcome and we settled down to a long, cold, wet, windy transit of one of the most unique and frightening places on earth.

▲ One of the most frustrating repairs! Mainsail down to fix a broken batten

Photo: © Jean-Baptiste Epron

◀ Congestion in cockpit

▶ Overleaf... Carving tracks – heading south

Photo © Jean-Baptiste Epron

Photo: © Jean-Baptiste Epron

'With the sighting of our first albatross the real
meat of the voyage was about to begin.'

CHASING the DAWN

Log 9

I have obviously passed this
island before but never knew
it existed. We had been
about 25 miles/40 kilometers
away and never saw it.

There is no defined latitude that separates the Southern Ocean from the South Atlantic, or the Indian from the Pacific oceans, but for sailors the divide is at roughly 40° S. For me the real distinctiveness of the Southern Ocean is the sea between Antarctica and the southern capes – at the latitude of Cape Horn. The Southern Ocean really begins below 56° S. For many sailors, however, the Southern Ocean is defined by something more esoteric: it's the wind, waves, wildlife and the sense of total isolation. It's a place of immense beauty and one that strikes fear into the hearts of mariners. During the Whitbread Race it was all of the above but my most vivid memories were of the incredible sailing. I was now looking forward to sailing here on *Orange*. With the sighting of our first albatross the real meat of the voyage was about to begin.

On 18 March we passed the island of Tristan da Cunha and I wrote:

See Log 9

The last land we had seen was the southwest corner of Madeira. After 16 days at sea we were ready to see something solid but it wasn't to be. Instead we were treated to some excellent sailing. A steady northwesterly wind was pushing us towards the Cape of Good Hope at between 20 and 25 knots. The forecast was for the wind to remain in the same quarter for several days and we were starting to lop off the miles at a rapid rate. 'These are free miles,' I said to Hervé as we sat and watched the white wake streaming out behind the boat. We had worked hard for every mile in the South Atlantic but now we were down south we were literally eating up the miles with little effort. Bruno calculated that we had already used more than 1,100 pounds/500 kilograms of food and fuel, and the boat was starting to feel lighter and more responsive. If we could keep this up, Gilles figured we might be able to beat the *Ushant* to Cape of Good Hope record. Our main objective was to beat *Sport Elec's* time around the world and while it was tempting to go after some of the other records along the way, we knew it would be foolish to take our eye off the main prize and potentially damage the boat for the sake of breaking a lesser record.

Jo Jo wrote in his log:

... onboard we've been feeling the South approach for several days now. The light's changing, the colour of the sea too. The variations in air and water temperature are surprising, more or less 10° C in several hours. With the cold and damp, it's sure that our rhythm of life will soon be changing.

▸ Heading into the infamous
Southern Ocean

CHASING the DAWN

Log 10

Had a tough few days, with broken headboard car and we twice broke the bottom batten in the mainsail. Thus no report yesterday as timing didn't quite work. Seemed like every time I went to write the wind dropped, increased, shifted in direction dramatically or we broke something. Was feeling pretty knackered last night but a lot better today. Quite a bit of swell around so there is some strong wind close by.

Once into the Southern Ocean we knew it would not be long before we got hammered by one of the many low-pressure systems that circulate around Antarctica. We needed the cold fronts to propel us around the bottom of the world, but at the same time we did not need too much wind. Maxicats like 20 to 25 knots of wind from behind. Any more than that and we would have to reduce sail without any increase in speed, and the danger of breaking the boat rises exponentially. One of our biggest fears was pitchpoling – going head over heels. Above a certain wind speed (which we figured was about 70 to 80 knots) the boat could become tumbleweed. The windage of the mast alone would be enough for the wind to pick the boat up and toss us wherever it liked. In any event we were concerned about ploughing into the wave ahead of us at the bottom of a long surf, so Gilles and Bruno were seeking out areas of more moderate winds.

Progress had speeded up again and we were back in full wet weather gear with spray and waves breaking across the decks. It was a simple and very satisfying life, carving off the miles on a course directly towards the first of the great southern capes, the Cape of Good Hope – Cap de Bonne Espérance as the French would say. A number of small breakages only slightly hampered our progress but caused great concern. It was hard work making these all too frequent repairs, and we had not yet experienced our first Southern Ocean storm.

 See Log 10

A few days into the Southern Ocean Gilles pointed out an intense low pressure on the weather chart:

There is a low pressure zone to the south generating very powerful winds. To the north there is isn't enough wind and we have no interest in getting mixed up with winds that are too strong, so for now our plan is to ride the corridor of wind between the high to the north and the approaching low without getting too close to the low.

With the low still some distance away, we were enjoying the sailing and *Orange* was flying. Jean-Baptiste's log summed up the feelings of all the crew:

Since yesterday morning it has been pure joy. The sea is at last in the right direction and we are bowling along at great speed. Orange the Marseille (her home port) is a very reassuring boat. Of course at high speed and manoeuvering demands enormous vigilance. Crossing the net from one hull to the other is a perilous business. You clip on your harness and alert the helmsman before any movement on the nets.

▸ Large ocean swells

In addition to his regular duties as one of the crew, Jean-Baptiste was also the cameraman on board:

I'm getting a lot of pleasure out of being the cameraman on board. When I am not on the winches I look more like a real tourist with all those cameras around my neck.

As we drove further south an odd thing happened. The water started to get warmer until it reached a high of 21° C. Suddenly we started to see flying fish along with albatrosses and petrels. Seeing all these together was an incredible and rare sight but the warm water didn't last long. We passed the Greenwich Meridian and the seas got colder again. And then the wind started to build. At first we had a steady 30 knots of wind and we were managing almost 30 knots of boat speed with a single reef in the main, staysail and medium gennaker. We moved everything in the boat aft to keep the stern down in the water and to try to keep the bow from digging in as we hurtled down the front of the waves. The forecast was for the wind to build to around 40 to 45 knots, but it's hard to predict exact speeds in that part of the world. In other places there are land stations or sea buoys that transmit the exact wind speed but not down here. It's as much a guessing game as it is science.

The low-pressure systems in the southern hemisphere rotate in a clockwise direction and track from west to east. It was important for the centre of the low to pass to the south of us; that way we could be sure of getting winds from behind. Should a low pass to the north of us we would get headwinds, something we wanted dearly to avoid. Fortunately, with our incredible speed, we could position ourselves relative to the low, and in some cases we actually outran them. This particular low was having a hard time catching us but we were starting to worry that it might catch up somewhere over the Agulhas Bank south of South Africa. The Agulhas Bank is an area of relatively shallow water, and big storms over shallow water spell trouble for any kind of yacht, not just high-speed catamarans. As the low got closer we set about preparing the boat. It's pretty exciting preparing your machine for a blow especially in the pitch black of night. The crew's attitude changes from light-hearted to very much more serious. There was no chatter, just pure concentration with minimal discussion.

As the low passed below us we expected a change in wind direction. As it approached the wind would be from the north and northwest. Once we were on the backside of the system we would have to gybe as the wind backed into the west and eventually southwest. We were all well rested and well fed, and in a way we were looking forward to our first big blow.

◀ Moving sails aft during a set-up change in preparation for 'The Storm'

Log 11

Average speed since the start 17.47 knots
The wind has been steadily increasing throughout the day into the high 20s and 30s. 30+ boat speed right now, the sea pattern is a little confused so the ride is unpredictable. We are still sailing with one reef in the mainsail, staysail and medium gennaker. Our next sail choices as the wind increases are tied to the cockpit. Everything else is now inside the boat as far back as possible. The forecast is slightly split. One forecast shows our expected wind speed at 45 knots, another map says 55 knots max. The approach is to hang onto the sails and wind that we have for as long as we can maintain a reasonable control margin. The thought of flipping over is now consistently on our minds.
We are trying to outrun the core of an approaching storm. We will certainly have a bit on our plate in the next few days!

 *See Log 11*

On 21 March at 0216 GMT we crossed from the South Atlantic Ocean into the South Indian Ocean and in doing so set a new record for the fastest time from Ile d'Ouessant to the Cape of Good Hope. It was a small but well-deserved victory and we savoured the moment. *Sport Elec* had taken 21 days to get there. Peter Blake and the crew of *ENZA* set a record of 19 days and 17 hours. We passed over the imaginary line due south from Cape Town in a new record time of 18 days, 18 hours and 40 minutes taking 23 hours and 13 minutes off *ENZA's* time.

Then the Roaring Forties started to roar. The low pressure that we had been keeping an eye on caught us up and the wind built rapidly. 'There's no doubt, we're in it now,' said Bruno over the satellite phone to our mission control base on a barge on the River Seine in Paris. Our land-based communication agency, Mer et Media, told the world of our situation:

The voice sounded far away and you could make out the sound of screaming water as it rushed along the maxi catamaran's side. During the radio bulletin today, Friday 22 March, Bruno was concentrated. He was listening as much to our questions as he was to the shouts coming

▲ Inspecting all equipment in preparation for our first real storm

from up on deck. The wind is blowing at around 50 miles/80 kilometres per hour and you have to be extremely vigilant both at the helm and with the trim of the sails. The boys are harnessed on, the helmsman watches the wave ahead as he catches it up, then rides it over while the deck watch have their hands glued to the sheets just in case they have to do an emergency dump. The atmosphere is tense and you have to shout to make yourself heard over the noise of shrieking wind and the waves as they explode on the bows and through the trampoline nets. 'We had an absolutely lousy sea last night,' Bruno told us. 'We've been in 45 knots of wind since last night! Otherwise all is well aboard.'

The maxi-catamaran Orange crossed some pretty inhospitable territory last night. Apart from having to cope with the wind, the giant had to confront the Agulhas current that descends down the coast of Africa whipping up a nasty boat breaking sea. And with the nasty sea comes another pitfall: the Agulhas shelf. This continental shelf off the coast of Africa stops the Atlantic swell because the sea bed rises from more than 16,500 feet/5,000 metres to only 2,526 feet/770 metres. This acts like a cauldron and the danger is omnipresent. 'We went down the mine a bit violently in a surf at about 0800 this morning,' continued Bruno. 'We are

▲ A concentrated Bruno finding a safe balance on the helm as the wind quickly builds

© Jean-Baptiste Epron

constantly at between 20 and 32 knots and this time we must have gone from 30 knots to 15 instantly. And with the inertia everything went flying around inside. Vlad was preparing a meal and he redecorated the galley. I split my lip open falling over and Florent hurt his pelvis. We called Dr Jean-Yves Chauve (our shore-based doctor) on the telephone and at the moment Florent is lying down and resting.'

See Log 12

Benoit Briand recounted his recent stint behind the wheel:

Helming in these conditions, there are many times when you lose contact with the boat for 10 seconds or so, as you are completely covered in water. You're not on the water any more but under it.

Gilles Chiorri gives another:

On my watch, I had 56 knots of wind and a 36-knot surf. Its tough, damp, violent and physical! I've never sailed down waves so fast. The speedometer had freaked out! Right now with our ski goggles on we look more like characters out of star wars than sailors!

The storm continued to gather strength relentlessly through the day. Updates on the system were relayed to those on deck. Conversation is now made by yelling at the top of your voice, repeating the information several times until it is received. Everyone is on edge. Trying to rest below is impossible; lying around in cold wet Gore-Tex has you shivering within minutes. Your ears are tuned in to the sounds of the hull and your heart skips a few beats every time a voice pierces the wind. Every time we accelerate everybody braces for a sudden stop as the beams plough into the cold sea.

The shuffle of feet on deck and the opening of the hatch was all it took to have all hands at the foot of the companionway ready to assist the on-deck team. The call was for yet more reduction of sail. This reduction would leave us with only a triple-reefed main. Working on the tramp was marginal: one second you were 33 feet/10 metres above the sea, the next you were under water. Our safety relied on the strength of the harness lines and their anchor points. If either failed we would be immediately swept off the deck into the cold, dark, wild sea, never to be seen again. The situation was very risky but everyone got on with the job, backing each other up, protecting and looking out for one another. A long wet wrestle and the storm jib was lashed to the beam. We all turned and scrambled back to the cockpit.

Log 12

```
Dawn was very welcome this
morning. We have been copping
a bit of a hammering. We are
trying to keep the boatspeed
down to the low 20s but
sometimes she just takes off.
The call comes out 'tenez-
vous' (hang on) and we brace
ourselves for a big stuff.
The waves are cresting in
small peaks that are very
unpredictable. It sets off a
succession of explosions of
water as these peaks hit the
hull and beams randomly.
Their next location is
unpredictable. Crossing the
tramp is a nightmare. Those
on deck are getting hammered.
It's a pretty wild ride and
very uncomfortable. People
are sleeping on sails in the
bilge still clad in full wet
weather gear waiting for a
call up to assist on deck.
Life's pretty 'full-on' right
now.
```

Those of us off watch gathered under the cuddy and talked about the situation. The change in sail area didn't seem to have helped and we were still surfing too, hard and fast. There was no other way to slow the boat down and we were at the mercy of the sea. We had lost control of the situation. Bruno came on deck and stood beside Hervé at the helm. The seas were getting bigger and bigger, so big that it was becoming too dangerous to take the drop down the face of the waves as the risk of cart-wheeling was too high. Other crew members crowded under the canopy. I was halfway down below when I felt the boat turning sharply. 'Oh my god, we are about to capsize,' I thought. I turned aorund to see both Hervé and Bruno wrestling with the wheel. Someone yelled in French and Ronnie clipped his harness onto the mainsheet and ran towards the foot of the mast. I scrambled on deck as we came head to wind. The wind was just howling. I jumped out of the cockpit onto the trampoline to help Ronnie. I had not clipped on and was immediately smacked by a huge wave. I was engulfed completely and knew I was airborne. 'Oh no, I am off the boat!,' I thought. Then the water subsided and I landed on the trampoline. I immediately scrambled on all fours to the little shelter behind the mid beam. I took a few deep breaths, thanked my lucky stars, clipped onto the mainsheet and ran forward again.

When I got to the mast, Ronnie had begun to release the main halyard, dropping the sail completely – the only sail we had left flying. I climbed onto the sail and began lashing it to the boom. Ronnie and Yann also climbed onto the sail while Yves, Vlad and Pépêche threw lines to us and we tied them off. We were now side onto the waves and wind, in a very vulnerable position. Looking back at Bruno on the helm, the waves were the biggest I had even seen, even at the movies! The windage of the hulls and wing mast was great enough to leave our windward hull suspended as an enormous wave passed beneath us. Thick spray burst through the trampoline engulfing us all. When it blew clear the hull was still suspended in the screaming wind. We were not in a good position if she had gone over. We finished lashing down the sail and scurried back to the cockpit. We were getting close to that 70 to 80 knots of wind that can flip one of these boats at the dock. Our next step would have been to flood the hulls with water making the boat heavier and hopefully more stable. We put off this option for as long as possible because of the effort involved in getting the water out again, and because of the extra stress the added weight gives to the structure. 'We have to get away from this system,' yelled Gilles.

23 March, Day 21
During the radio chat session with mission control Bruno said:

We'll not forget Friday–Saturday night in a hurry. It's not every day you find yourself under bare poles on a 33m boat. Even the crew that have done The Race have never seen that before. We shortened sail until there was nothing at all. None of this stopped us from making 20+ knots with just the mast! What surprised us most was the force of the sea. We managed to have a life raft torn away from the aft beam overnight! We can see the waves coming about 500–700 metres off. We take avoiding action, which turns out not to work and we find ourselves at the foot of a wall of water. Speed, no speed, go through it, cut across it? You have to make your mind up quickly. Once you have decided what you're going to do, there's no going back on it. You're generally in for a wet, violent down hill ride. With no guarantee as to how you're going to land. That's known as surf, performed on a 20-ton boat which looks pretty much like a cork on the surface of the ocean.

With the boat parked I went below to try and send off a report via email. The noise of the waves breaking over the boat and crashing into the sides was indescribable. As was the motion. I kept getting thrown about the cabin and was wondering if it was all worth it when suddenly I received an email of encouragement from my sister and niece. It's amazing how a few words of encouragement can change your world. The note also bought a sudden twinge of homesickness. I had been away for too long already. For the next 18 hours we huddled in the dark, cold bilges of our craft. The sounds of the screaming winds and roaring seas left us bracing ourselves against nature's anger and fury. Our lifeline was being battered and we heavily contemplated our fate and the possible end to our journey...

At mid morning on 24 March, on our 22nd day at sea, we broke free of that storm, some 1,000 miles/1,600 kilometres south of the Kerguelen Islands, and resumed our course to the southeast, towards a new dawn and a new day. During the storm I remember saying 'for every tough day at sea, there are at least five great days in return'. Well, just then we were ready to cash in.

◀ The situation getting serious
Photo: © Jean-Baptiste Epron

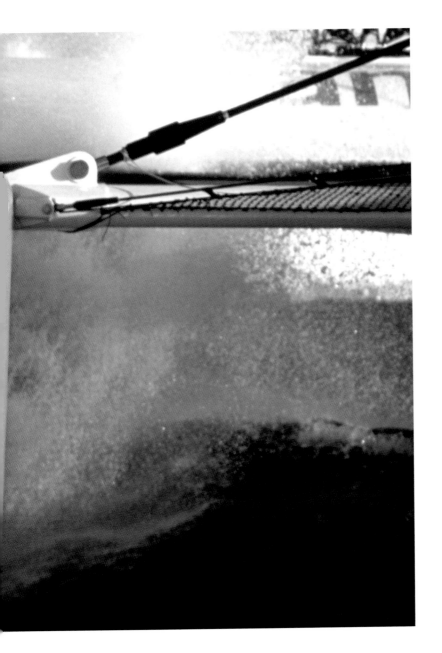

'The passage below Australia was a very special time for me. I had now been away from home for about 14 months and this was the closest I was going to get for a while yet.'

By the time we were completely free of the system, we were past the Kerguelen Islands, a remote group midway between Africa, Antarctica and Australia. Kerguelen is a French possession, much to the satisfaction of the crew. Even though we would not be stopping, they felt a little bit closer to home knowing that a little piece of their country was nearby. The island group has had an interesting but bloody history. Bloody certainly for the abundant wildlife that inhabit the waters around the islands: American and British sealers lived on the islands in the late 18th century, depleting the fur seal colonies to such a degree that by the early 19th century there were only a handful left. Penguins and elephant seals met a similar fate. The sealers moved on only to be replaced by whalers. In 1908 the first whaling licence was granted, but the waters south of Kerguelen yielded little and whaling was abandoned in 1911.

During World War II, the Allies were worried that the fjord-like inlets of the islands could be used as enemy submarine bases and consequently mined them, and Kerguelen was left to the scientists. France was obliged to occupy the island in order to retain sovereignty and, in December 1949, a temporary base was established at Port-aux-Français. Since then Kerguelen has been occupied solely by scientists with a population varying between 50 and 100 people. The base is large and well appointed, with a hospital, restaurant, library, sports centre, cinema and chapel. The fur seal colonies and penguin rookeries have since recovered and provide ample material for study. The archipelago was yet another reminder of the many extraordinary places we sailed right past.

Shortly after the Kerguelens we ran into another tactical dilemma for Bruno and Gilles. A huge high-pressure system had filled to the west of the islands and, being on the eastern side of the high, we were getting strong southerly winds. The southerly winds themselves were not a problem. The problem was another intense low evolving to the northeast of the Kerguelens and with the strong southerly winds we were not able to drive south to get clear of the approaching system. 'There must be a mousehole somewhere,' Bruno noted. 'It's up to us to find it.'

Eric Mas, our weather expert at Meteo Consult, summed up the situation:

This weather system is very complicated. Orange is going through an exceptionally complex system between highs and lows. As long as the sea has not settled down and coming from the right direction, Orange cannot anticipate the evolution of the low pressure as we would wish. A race against the clock has started to avoid the catamaran again coming up against very strong and badly oriented winds in a few days time.

▶ Yves working at the goose neck in the dark

We needed to find some smooth sailing so that we could position ourselves for the next big storm.

While Bruno worried about the weather, those of us on deck were dealing with the brutally cold conditions. The southerly winds were blowing right off the Antarctic ice and were making working on deck very difficult. When we wanted to do anything we had to take our gloves off and within seconds our hands would be almost frozen. Still, I was enjoying the adventure. I loved knowing that much of the rest of the world was asleep, tucked up some place warm and dry, while we were wet and cold running through the spray trying to squeeze a few more miles out of the record. I'm not trying to sound hard-core; it's just that I enjoyed feeling that what we were doing was different and adventurous.

A trip like ours, racing against an imaginary competitor, was not something I had done before. My experience had been of racing against tangible opposition whose tactics we could study and attempt to outwit whilst we were all dealing with the same weather conditions at the same time. Racing against *Sport Elec* was a different story altogether. They had sailed this way years before and had experienced quite different conditions from those we were experiencing. They had their share of problems and difficult situations, but I did wonder if our late start had made it more difficult for us.

Each day Mer et Media would put out a press release that summed up the day's news. At the top of the press release they would list the number of days we had been racing, the number of days we needed to finish within to beat the record, and an estimate of how far we were ahead of the record. Since we had been ahead of *Sport Elec's* time almost since Day 1, they listed an estimated distance we were ahead, not behind. Of course it was speculative, so I was not too surprised when Olivier de Kersauson took issue with our calculations.

For me the ghost tracks of past competitors on our course were only a point of a reference. Sometimes used as a confidence boost, other times used as a kick in the pants. This record attempt had a beginning and an end. The rest was irrelevant. If we managed to sail across that finish line without assistance or stopping then we would have set a time taken to complete the voyage. This might be the fastest recorded time or the third or fourth fastest. If we could not finish the course, for whatever reason, we would have failed. We were to be reminded constantly of the possibility of failure.

The relentless pounding by the waves was starting to take its toll on the boat. The aft beam was beginning to show signs of delamination . A big crack in the outer skin and two of the interior bulkheads that supported the beam were breaking away. Yves Le Blévec first noticed the problem. He was sitting in the aft video room in the port hull and looked through the escape hatch into the aft beam. The honeycomb core had collapsed and both the inner and outer skins had started to peel apart. Fibres of carbon were beginning show on the outside of the beam.

Fortunately the problem was caught early; Yves and Philippe got straight to work. They cleaned the whole area, and laminated a patch onto the inside of the beam. They mended the cracked bulkheads, and through-bolted and glued a piece of carbon over the delaminated area, to a backing plate inside the beam. It was a tough job, not only because of the size of the job, but also because of the conditions under which they were working. We were sailing at 20 knots while they were wedged into the aft beam with the fumes and dust. In order to create the necessary conditions for the resin to set they diverted heater ducts into the beam. Getting this sort of damage was alarming. We all knew that the crack could still grow and that if it did we would be forced to retire for reasons of safety. We withheld news of the damage for several days until the repair had been completed and we were confident that it was holding.

Meanwhile we were still trying to find a gap that would allow us to sail south, away from the approaching low. The seas were very confused and were coming from three different directions. They eventually settled down a little allowing us to dive a bit deeper into the Southern Ocean. Bruno summed up the situation during the morning chat show:

We started the night with a nice and tidy sea. But having dropped down to the southeast as planned we have found a cross sea that has forced us to slow down somewhat.

Hervé Jan picked up the explanation:

With 25 knots of wind and a flat sea these boats can easily go the speed of the wind. But in a rough sea you have to adapt yourself to the sea state if you don't want to break anything.

With the new cross-sea we tappered back a bit on our speed by shortening sail to a triple-reefed main and staysail. Despite the reduced configuration we were still knocking off day's runs of 500+ miles/800 kilometres.

◀ Taking a reef
▲ Yves formulating another repair strategy
▲ Philippe laminating inside back beam
▶ Overleaf... The view through the escape hatch that allowed Yves to identify the damage to the back beam

115

Log 13

See Log 13

Had a shocker last night. Tore a seam in my wet weather pants and ended up with a soaked crotch. I am now sporting bright yellow dry suit, I hope it's the fashion colour for April!

At the end of March we were approaching the longitude of Cape Leeuwin, the second of the great capes we were leaving well to port. Peter Blake and Robin Knox-Johnston and the crew on *ENZA* still held the fastest time from Ushant to Cape Leeuwin. For us to break their record we would have to pass south of the Cape no later than Sunday 31 March at 2327 GMT. My focus and excitement was directed at the rate at which we were approaching Australia.

Just as we neared Australia we headed even further south and for the first time since the start we were below 50° S. Bruno announced:

We've just crossed the Antarctic convergence zone. The water is at 4° C, the temperature that icebergs like.

With that bit of news we started an iceberg watch. The radar was running full time and the entire team on watch was alerted to look out for ice. The problem with icebergs was not the actual bergs; the real issue was the growlers or bits that break off. They can be about the size of the average

▲ Bows sniffing
▸ Typical conditions when travelling at over 25 knots

Log 14

Gidday Australia from ice berg country. During the early part of last evening we crossed the longitude of Cape Leeuwin, Western Australia. We are now officially under Australia and its great to see it on the chart.

It's now sunrise here and we have had an amazing night's sailing. Clearish skies and long drawn out waves. 30 knots of wind and 25 knots of boat speed. We were also treated to the greatest display of the Aurora Australis that I have ever seen. I have seen the phenomenon many times but never so clear or brilliant. We are quite deep south, in the 50s and south of the Antarctic Convergence Zone. Water temperature is below 5º C so we are expecting to encounter ice at some stage. It had always been the plan to stay away from ice for as long as possible but we will see what the next few days have in store for us. It's all a bit concerning on such a boat but on the other hand I don't want the lads that have not seen these amazing frozen islands to go home without a clear image in their memory.

The instruments that compute and record our wind speed, direction and angle are not working at the moment which makes steering in the dark difficult.

Had a 'monty' two nights ago when the wind shifted its direction by 40º and we were suddenly sailing hard into a seaway. Setting up to gybe was a mission. Everyone being thrown around on the tramp. You know when you are sieving flour or dirt and continued...

car but that is the only thing average about them – they can be deadly. Hit one of them and we would sink just as fast as if we had hit the main iceberg. Growlers mostly float just below the surface, when they were above they looked like just another breaking wave, making them very difficult to spot, especially from the deck of a catamaran screaming through a dark night.

 See Log 14

A major present for all of us was another record to add to our growing list: we passed the longitude of Cape Leeuwin, the most southerly tip of Western Australia, 29 days, 7 hours and 22 minutes after passing Ushant. Despite our troubled times in the Indian Ocean we had taken 8 hours and 39 minutes off the time set by *ENZA* five years earlier. Crossing the southern Indian Ocean had been costly – the time spent hove-to and sailing under reduced sail to baby the boat had set us back a little – but despite this we were a full day and seven hours faster to Cape Leeuwin than *Sport Elec*. It's interesting to note that we crossed the line of longitude which passes through Cape Leeuwin at almost the same latitude as *Sport Elec* had done when they set the record. We were actually 50 miles further south, which on an ocean of this scale was fairly minimal.

Bruno was neither happy nor discouraged by our progress to date:

Compared with the Jules Verne record we have lost a little of our lead sailing across the Indian Ocean. We attacked a bit too hard when entering the Indian Ocean and we put plenty of horsepower and energy into it. But it didn't pay. And then we were a bit under canvassed while we tried to figure out what to do.

All in all we had had a great month of sailing. The fact that we had been ahead of *Sport Elec* since the start, and that we had not had ideal conditions, left me happy with our progress. We were fit, happy, sailing fast, and best of all we were below Oz.

The following day was 1 April, April Fool's Day. We shied away from practical jokes onboard but on land things were slightly different. A leading American sailing news website published the following article written by Herb McCormick, a journalist, who had crewed with us during the fourth stage of our victorious EDS Atlantic Challenge race on *Kingfisher*.

A journalist in France republished the article on the 2 April after some real news, sparking a bit of frenzy amongst those following our voyage.

April Fool's joke

Creaming through the Southern ocean in quest of the Trophee Jules Verne for fastest non-stop circumnavigation, Bruno Peyron's mega-catamaran *Orange* has made a serious detour. And the big cat is now minus one crewmember.

Yesterday, Peyron made an unscheduled pit-stop off the Southern Ocean outpost of Kerguelen Island to deposit Australian sailor Nick Moloney, who was dismissed unceremoniously after a pair of related incidents that began last Friday morning. Moloney was at the helm when *Orange* performed an all-standing jibe in a fierce westerly gale, blowing out three battons and almost pitchpoling the boat. Moloney compunded the problem when, in an attempt to make light of the incident, he told Peyron he was "trying to dodge an ice flow in the shape of a rabbit." Superstitious French sailors do not allow the word "rabbit" to be uttered on a boar at sea.

"At that point," said Peyron "I had no choice but to nuke Nick."

Orange turned around and pounded upwind for two days into the teeth of the gale, losing time and miles in their bid to topple the record set by Olivier de Kersauson's *Sport-Elec* in 1997. Peyron also responded to a press release issued by de Kersauson last week accuisng Peyron of putting an overly optimistic spin on his position updates. "De Kersauson may attach his lips to my petite derriere," said Peyron.

Moloney, who was the only non-French crewmember aboard *Orange* was put ashore on Kerguelen Island late Sunday night. Now he faces another problem. He is the only non-French resident on an island inhabited by 27 French research scientists, all men, several of whom seemed inordinately pleased to have a handsome, strapping Australian sailor suddenly deposited in their midst. The next Kerguelen re-supply vessel is not due for 11 weeks. "Tout alors," said Moloney, who did not appear to have made progress with his ongoing French lessons. "I think I am in the deep merde."

the big pieces are left bouncing around on the mesh? That's sort of what it gets like. The situation occurred so quickly that not many of the guys had their harnesses on. It was pretty full on for a period until we took a reef and gybed. Wild times. Repair to the back beam is finished so we will continue to monitor. The damage was not really surprising, the water hits that area like a sledgehammer and we have been hit by a few big waves over the past nine days. Its very cold as you can imagine but it feels like we have been making better progress over the past 24 hours. I will enjoy watching Australia and New Zealand pass by to our north, we can then focus on Cape Horn. I think most onboard are enjoying the Southern Ocean, so far, which is a little strange. I seem to be setting a trend in my yellow dry suit, as more appear every watch change.

I've been receiving many mails onboard from the web site and am amazed by how many people are living this adventure with us.

I have a warm sleeping bag waiting for me in the other hull – three hours of bliss ahead.

Last off watch we celebrated Seb Josse's 27th birthday with ham and balloons; all through the night there were loud bangs as people stood on stray balloons in the dark. Makes everyone jump a little on a boat with tons of load on everything.

The passage below Australia was a very special time for me. I had now been away from home for about 14 months and this was the closest I was going to get for a while yet. For the next few days I could look north and dream of home and being with my family. I was still thousands of miles away but being in the general area made me feel a little closer to my roots. I thought of my mum, living on the floor in the study, getting up in the middle of the night to log on to the net to check our progress. She would have the mouse in one hand and her rosary beads in the other as she watched us sail by a thousand miles to the south. Philippe Pépêche lived in Fremantle and he too could be found looking north as we sailed past his home:

It's true, I was thinking about my little family, and I even had a look when I was on deck to see if I could see the lights of the car.

Our arrival in Aussie waters was memorable for the rest of the crew as well. The spectacular show of the southern lights, the Aurora Australis, continued for many nights, dancing across clear starry skies. This giant light show crossed the sky fading through green and yellow and back to green again – just spectacular – and with the night air so crisp and clear

▲ So close yet so far... passing 600 miles south of my home in Australia

Photo: © Jean-Baptiste Epron

▸ Just cruzin

Log 15

250 miles/400 kilometers
from the longitude of
Tasmania and a little over
1,000 miles/1600 kilometers
to the half way mark. The
skies have been clear with a
few strong squalls to add a
bit of spice. Orange is well
maintained and the standard
of living onboard is great.
We all clean the interior
regularly and everybody
appears to be organised with
their personal stuff. It
varies from some guys with
what looks like a sack full
of dirty washing, to some
with everything sealed in
zip lock bags labled and
placed neatly in their
locker. Nevertheless we are
not tripping over each
other's stuff which is a
good change from most boats.
Having trouble trying to get
through this email as am
constantly having to dash on
deck as squalls form and
pass us by. Just did an
interview with a breakfast
show in Canberra, Australia.
Was fantastic to hear some
Aussie voices. I am now all
smiles.
We are awaiting dawn. Should
pass Tasmania sometime today
at a distance of the
Sydney-Hobart race further
south. Australia will then
be behind us.

it was magic on deck sitting and watching nature in all its glory. The sea also opened up allowing us to pile on speed. We could make 30 knots of boat speed without too much stress to either the crew or the boat. *Orange* took a nose dive a few times but fortunately there were no more injuries. We had all been listening to the harmonics from the hull and appendages, and were more in tune with the speed below by the sounds. We knew when to brace ourselves for a sudden stop. I was on deck for one of the latest bow plants and watched as the whole boat was engulfed in an explosion of spray. Spectacular to watch and an extraordinary experience but not to be recommended; the strain on gear and nerves is too much.

Australia seemed to be sliding by so fast, I was a little disappointed:

 *See Log 15*

I spoke to many journalists while we were below Australia, and sometimes I would be put on hold briefly as I was transferred to the studio. The backing sound whilst I waited was usually the live feed from the studio. I was often on air after the weather or a traffic report, or occasionally the news. It was amazing for me to hear everyday radio from all parts of Australia, including the Outback, and to speak Australian to Australians. I know that this sounds crazy but remember that I had been at sea for a long time, with 12 Frenchmen, in our own little world where the official language was French. The journalists were probably surprised at how talkative I was. I look back on that period with fond memories and thank them all for taking an interest in our story and sharing it with my fellow countrymen and women.

The waters below Australia treated us well, especially in comparison with the Indian Ocean. In his morning radio schedule Bruno was relaxed and pleased with life on board:

At the moment it's very pleasant. We are almost getting free miles. The boat is sliding along easily and not suffering. Conditions below are even dry which does everyone good.

True. Our bunks were warm and dry, and they were a perfect refuge from sailing the boat. We all looked forward to time off when we could pile into our sleeping bags, and get warm and comfortable for a few hours, putting aside the cares of recordbreaking and holding the boat together. Even life on deck had improved as Yann Eliès explained:

The organisation of the watch depends on conditions on deck. If it's warm we are all four in the cockpit. If it's cold or if the sailing is quiet, we try to spare the crew as much as possible with just the helmsman and a single crewman on the sheets. The other two crew are huddled in the cuddy out of the spray and icy wind that's coming straight out of the fridge!

While we were eating up the miles our thoughts started to turn to the halfway mark, somewhere between Australia and New Zealand. As we ripped past Tasmania the conversation was dominated by this topic. I was a bit wary of thinking about being 'half way'. There was so much ahead of us and so many things that could potentially go wrong. Too many hurdles. 'Time to start crossing those fingers and toes,' I wrote in one email. We were still sailing full on, *Orange* literally shredding the miles and the crew hanging on as we hurtled through the dark nights at 30 knots. It was almost unreal. To be this far from the start, going this fast, on this boat with these amazing guys was something I could hardly imagine. I thought back to the days sailing on the Barwon River, to our happy hut and the sandbank I used to sail to as a kid, and I could not help but think that I was one of the luckiest guys in the world.

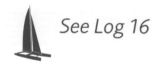 *See Log 16*

Log 16

Around midnight local time we crossed the halfway point of our course in longitude. A very special moment for us all. A different mindset for everybody already. Progress has been great but this morning the squalls lost their punch and the wind is shifting to the west and dropping in strength. Sometimes I feel like I am getting a cold so I hope I am wrong.

I am happy to be watching our westerly longitude reduce every hour. It's an amazing tour, one that I will be a little sad to finish. It's crazy, sometimes I feel like I could stay out here forever but there's a goal and we need to keep pushing the miles aside. One day I may do such a trip without a goal or destination.

▶ Overleaf... Crests of waves skimming through the trampoline as we prepare to hoist a smaller headsail

CHAPTER 8

'On our 43rd day at sea Cape Horn suddenly
appeared out of the rain. We were all on
deck to witness the sight of land,
our first since Madeira.'

Log 17

As I write I am completely on edge. We are doing 33 to 35 knots, the new watch has just taken over and I honestly feel like we are out of control. I am sitting with my feet braced against the bulkhead really just waiting to plunge into a pit and stop.

We are experiencing some strong squall activity again. We have a bit of a stressful cocktail mixing here. We are deep in the Southern Ocean in strong winds and steep waves. We are sailing at a boat speed continually in excess of 30 knots. We are now losing the moon and heading straight for an ice field!

Right now is probably a good time to say a big hello to my mates currently in New Zealand training for the America's Cup. Good on ya! Right now I am thinking of making a comeback to short course day sailing. Na, not really, I love this action.

We hurtled into the second half of the voyage at full speed. South of New Zealand we surfed down a huge wave at 38.6 knots. A new top speed record and with the Aussie behind the wheel! The night was so dark I could hardly make out the horizon. If I had been able to see I probably wouldn't have steered the boat down a wave that big. But I did, and no sooner had I lined it up I felt the boat take off and knew that I was powerless to stop it. *Orange* started to slide down the front of the wave, the water shrieking as it ripped past the boat, the hulls vibrating from the speed. The ocean ahead seemed to open up, almost swallowing us as we charged towards the bottom. Horizontal hurricanes streamed off our bows, stretching into the darkness astern. All I could think of was what would happen if the bows dug in and we pitchpoled. The crew told me that if the record still stood when we arrived back in Brest I would have to buy dinner for the whole crew. A bit of a strange custom if you ask me, but who was I to argue? At least we had survived.

After my watch I went below to send an email

See Log 17

We were already down to two reefs in the mainsail and storm spinnaker; the next step would be dropping the spinnaker and taking another reef. Instead we just kept on flying through the dark night.

One of the problems associated with our late departure was the lack of daylight. The nights were longer than the days and the nights down south were pitch, pitch black. Often low cloud obliterated the stars and moon. With a dark night sky and dark ocean it was impossible to see where the sky ended and the water began. If we had hit a chunk of ice at those speeds we would have sunk before the guys below had a chance to get on deck – that's if they survived the impact.

To add to our stresses, a new gale was bearing down on us. The wind picked up to just below 50 knots and we were flying along, surfing in the mid-30s. 'We are really hauling,' Bruno yelled into the phone during the morning chat. The radio reception was scratchy and broken up forcing him to shout. We were entering a part of the world so far from anywhere that even the satellite coverage was minimal and it was about to fade altogether. For a few days we would only be in email contact with the outside world. To make matters worse we suddenly lost a day – we crossed the International Date Line and had to give back all those hours we had accumulated while sailing east. Crossing the Date Line was another symbolic day for us. It meant that we were now back in the western hemisphere and it felt good to be counting down the degrees to the finish, from 180° W to the Greenwich Meridian at 0°.

Orange was sailing 280 miles/450 kilometres south of the course taken by *Sport Elec*. We were really in the deep south and the relentless pounding on the boat was beginning to show. Patches of antifouling paint were starting to wear thin and there were some rust stains appearing. The patch to the aft beam was holding up but it was an indication of the wear and tear the boat was undergoing. The crew were doing marginally better. Some of the lads were suffering from skin irritations from being in wet weather gear for so long and there was a bit of tendonitis in some joints. My eye was healing after being smacked by a halyard tail a few days earlier, and despite the usual aches and pains I was in excellent health. The food had been great and with so much fresh air and exercise, who wouldn't feel good?

The Pacific was definitely milder than both the Indian and Atlantic oceans had been. A ridge of high pressure built ahead of us and Gilles and Bruno were trying to figure out a way to get past it. It was similar to the one that had blocked our way down the Atlantic: large and obtrusive with no way around it. Bruno decided that there was no way we could get underneath the system, so we headed north to get around the top,

▲ Fast sailing in the south
Photo: Orange *crew*

Log 18

Sky is grey, horizon is only
a few miles away due to the
mist and waves. Our angle to
the wind is getting better
which makes for faster
sailing speed. Our world is
pretty small but active.
Last night we were moving a
lead control for the
headsail. A few of the lads
were working on the tramp
and through the illumination
of their red headlamps I
could see that we were
travelling along as a ball
of liquid smoke. There was
thin spray continually
fizzing through the tramp
about twice the height of a
person.
News from my sister – Mum's
a bit stressed!
I have been stuffing my wet
thermals in the bottom of my
sleeping bag to dry them
with my body heat as I
sleep. I emptied it out
today and found one stray
sock and a toasty warm hat –
what a bonus!
2,700 miles/4,345 kilometres
to Cape Horn.
Everyone's taking bets at
how many days it's going to
take us to get to Cape Horn,
then how many in the
Atlantic. It's my birthday
on 5 May so my guess is that
we will finish then.

or at least across the top. As the barometer rose and the weather improved, each millibar brought a distinct improvement to life on board.

One morning I was at the helm running deep to slow the boat down while Philippe worked on the tack of the spinnaker. I was concentrating hard to make sure that I did not sweep him off with a big wave. The swells were really huge. I was watching this small figure descend metres and metres down the walls of water, the back faces of the waves in front, and then soar skyward as the sterns dipped into the troughs and our bows pushed up the waves. It was an incredible sight and it made me realise how small and vulnerable we were.

The temperature was mild considering it was late in the year and we were in the Southern Ocean. As we got over the top of the high pressure the wind headed us for a while, and we went hard on the wind for a few hours. The only tough part was dealing with the fact that we were hard on the wind in a region of the world where we should have been getting westerlies. Hervé yelled through the wind:

I cannot believe we are hard upwind so close to the bloody 50s.

Slowly the wind backed into the northwest and we eased sheets and started eating up the miles to Cape Horn again. The sky was grey with visibility of only a few miles as a heavy mist settled over the boat. We plunged further south again crossing the 50th parallel into the Antarctic Convergence Zone once more.

For a period we crashed our way towards small icons on our electronic charts. These icons marked iceberg sightings from yachts competing in the Volvo Ocean Race – a race around the world with crew and with stops, formerly the Whitbread. The fleet had been the last vessels to pass through this area, about two months before. The bergs do not move at great speed so even information this old was still fairly accurate and very important. That night we were to pass within 30 miles/48 kilometres of the first reported sighting.

 *See Log 18*

Dry clothing is like gold dust! For the voyage we packed four sets of thermals (top and bottom), one mid layer, one fleece top, four pairs of socks, one T-shirt, one pair of shorts, one sun hat and one warm woolly hat, one pair of gloves and one wet weather outer shell. We were also allowed boots for the cold and light shoes for warmer climates. I chose to take two pairs of boots, which is just as well because on entering the Southern Ocean, Ronnie discovered that his brand new boots leaked so I happily gave him my second pair.

The conditions started to set up perfectly for some incredible blasting. Everything began to fall into place, the wave, the wind angle and the sail combination. Bruno gave us the thumbs up to attack and we began carving; 600 miles/966 kilometres in 24 hours was suddenly an easy target. I remember taking the helm just before dawn thinking that the speed display must be over-reading: we were cruising along at 34 to 36 knots on a very smooth sea. The numbers came effortlessly to the point where you could have steered with just two fingers on the wheel. As the first signs of dawn began to cast light over our surroundings it became apparent from the way the water was ripping past that we were indeed smoking along.

If conditions like this were more frequent, who knows how short the round-the-world record could go. Unfortunately windows like this were few and far between, and a few days down-track this one came to an end.

▲ Wet and wild days in the Southern Ocean

Photo: © Jean-Baptiste Epron

Log 19

Under 2,000 miles 3,220
kilometres to Cape Horn. The
past two days have been very
fast. Last night we started
to encounter a seaway and
are now punching the bows in
every now and then, scooping
up a lot of water and
depressing speed. If we can
maintain our current speed
we could reach Cape Horn in
a little over three days.
Either way we are on our
final approach heading to
the Cape. We are now 55° S
and deep into ice territory.
Nothing to report yet but
its now just a matter of
time.
Current boat speed is 34
knots. It's quite bumpy. I
didn't sleep well last off
watch as the boat lurches
radically. It feels like the
helmsman is out of control
but says he's OK.
We are really starting to
drag the bows right now so I
had better get myself
somewhere a little more
secure before I get thrown
into a bulkhead by a sudden
stop.

See Log 19

The days blended into the nights and the nights back into days as we slowly closed on Cape Horn. Gilles Chiorri described the sailing in the daily radio chat:

The sky cleared momentarily and the light made the ocean look like liquid chrome. It's amazing how everything loses its colour down here. Our boat is bright orange and our dry suits are bright yellow yet everything looks very dull and grey. The only striking burst of colour is when a large wave will peak and before it crumbles its crest shines an incredible blue. The flashes of blue were constantly catching my eye and I marvelled at them. They were like small pieces of jewellery on an otherwise bleak landscape.

A group of us was gathered under the port canopy discussing icebergs when Florent casually came on deck, immediately looked around and came out with 'Icebergs like that one!' We could see in his eyes that he was focused on something. We all looked in the direction that he was looking to see a huge chunk of ice roll out of the mist right on our bow.

▲ Iceberg country
▶ Tough work changing sails in the
  cold

Photos: © Jean-Baptiste Epron

Log 20

Last night was radical to say the least. Absolutely freezing cold, rotating through our watch system with 30 minute stint at the helm, 30 minutes warming up, 30 minutes ice watch, 30 minutes warming up. Multiply this schedule by two and that was the complete four-hour watch.
Ice watch was insane. For 30 minutes you harnessed yourself to the mast standing on the rotator foot on the front side of the base of the mast. Holding onto two rope deflectors you attempt to distinguish growlers from breaking waves. All this time the helmsman is trying to obtain the greatest speed he can, sometimes sustaining 36 knots. The boat was just busting the seas apart. I remember thinking 'How the hell are we supposed to see anything with all this water flying about the place?' Poised to blow the storm jib halyard, as covered up as possible, my face was painfully cold. My feet were beginning to go numb from the cold so I began to dance to the tune New York, New York in an attempt to get warm. Not sure why I chose this song?
As the waves broke their crests cast a lighter glow on the dark sea. Your heart would skip a few beats before you could act or yell a warning: the mass was already beneath the tramp or bursting over the hulls. Twice I thought I saw large pieces of ice but there was nothing I could do. You just hang on that little bit tighter and brace for a high-speed collision. If this all sounds a little bit crazy - it was! Standby watch was a rolling watch monitoring the radar for large bergs.

It was about half a mile long, maybe a quarter of a mile wide, very tall with a flat top. The berg was about three miles ahead directly in our path. J-B was driving wearing a French firefighter's helmet to keep his head warm and to protect his eyes from the spray. He started yelling and pointing. We bore off sharply to slow down. Pépêche ran across the tramp to alert Bruno. We converged with the berg very quickly and within minutes had no option other than to pass the mass on its downwind side. Not the preferred side to pass icebergs as the small pieces, the growlers, that regularly break away and lie just below the water surface, usually get blown downwind. Every one immediately came on deck and we spread ourselves out around the boat looking for growlers in our path. We passed within a mile and a half of the mass. No one said a thing, but I am sure that we were all thinking the same thoughts. What would have happened if we had come across that floating island in the night? We immediately slowed down to 25 knots, if you can call that slow. We had been running the radar full time, but ironically it was off when we spotted the berg. Gilles was doing some work on the instrument system and all the electronics were shut off. I lay in my bunk that night thinking about the ice and the danger but mostly marvelling at what we had seen. How lucky we were to see the sights we were seeing. Many people read about icebergs and see them on television but how many actually get to see a giant iceberg in the middle of the ocean? Indeed we were lucky.

The general consensus onboard was that we needed to keep the speed on. Cutting down the amount of time in the Southern Ocean was figured to be safer than sailing slowly, so we stopped heading south for a while and put the pedal to the floor. The night ahead was one that I will never, ever forget.

 *See Log 20*

We were looking ahead to Cape Horn. On 11 April we passed the 'under-a-thousand-miles-to-go' (1,600 kilometres) point. At the rate we were sailing we had less than two days to go. *Orange* was averaging over 500 miles/800 kilometres a day, just loping across the ocean eating up the miles. I was looking forward to seeing the famous Cape again. The wind was blowing steadily from the north. Bruno's thoughts were on his rounding aboard *Explorer*:

I often think about 1993 when we were hit by a tropical low that neither the Americans nor the Chileans nor the Australians saw coming. It started at 40 knots peaking at 70 with gusts above 80 knots.

We knew that we would not be safely out of the Southern Ocean until we rounded the corner and turned the bows towards home.

We were not alone in this remote part of the world. A replica of the tall ship *Endeavour* was in the vicinity, though travelling much more slowly. It was en route from Australia to the Falkland Islands. I threatened the Frenchmen that if they gave me too much lip then I would call the Aussies onboard *Endeavour* to come over and kick their butts!

The weather in this region is very volatile and the conditions started to get really bad again. A small but strong system passed over us pushing the wind speed into the 50-knots range again creating a dangerous sea. At daybreak we dropped the main and sailed under bare poles and storm jib for a while. It's amazing how much windage the boat had with just the wing mast, tiny storm jib and the two hulls. The gusts were like being punched in the chest. We were wearing ski goggles on deck most of the time now as our eyes were getting pretty trashed after weeks of continual spray. We were still flying along while we made every attempt to slow the boat down. Fortunately the wind eased a little and we set the main again a few hours later. We pressed on towards gaucho country, towards the ultimate 'land's end'.

Excitement built throughout the evening and the next morning a foggy day dawned beyond *Orange*'s bows. Two miles to port, the sombre mass of Cape Horn could just be made out in the loom of the Chilean lighthouse. On our 43rd day at sea Cape Horn suddenly appeared out of the rain. We were all on deck to witness the sight of land, our first since Madeira. This was my second rounding of the great Cape – my first was during the Whitbread race in 1998. I was just as excited this time. There is something truly incredible about this part of the world with all its myths and legends. The low outline of the land was spotted just as the pale light of dawn lit the sky. The faint beam of the lighthouse could be seen struggling to pierce the poor visibility. We had passed the Diego Ramirez islands during the night and then gybed to approach the Horn on port tack. We tried to sail deep around the headland but were forced to gybe again quickly in strong winds as it became apparent that we were getting a little too close. In a frenzy we shortened sail and turned in a very rough seaway.

Ronnie has spent a lot of time cruising these waters and made contact with an old friend, the lighthouse keeper, via VHF radio. The wind was blowing at a steady 30 knots from the west. Seeing the Horn was a great relief but a different experience for all of us. For Hervé it was his seventh rounding.

A bulletin from our press centre in Paris read:

Saturday 13 April 2002. Orange has rounded the formidable Cape Horn – four days ahead of Olivier de Kersauson's 1997 time.

Bruno:
Rounding the Horn does not mean that our difficulties have come to an end. The main thing is that our boat is intact and we have sailed an impressive leg from Cape Leeuwin to Cape Horn: 12 days and 19 hours between the two.

Bruno knew, as did we all, that the leg up the Atlantic would be fraught with challenges. *Club Med* (our sistership) suffered most of its damage during The Race in the Atlantic, and Blake and company aboard *ENZA* got severely hammered a stone's throw from the finish. Sébastien Josse summed up the feelings of most of the crew:

The Horn will remain one of the highlights for me, even though we could only just see it. It was not quite so emotional as the times when we were sailing among the icebergs. But it does effect you since it is unique in the life of a sailor.

The PR people were talking about new records set but for me it was more than records and numbers. It was another of my dreams come true. Fair enough, we had set a new fastest time from Ushant to Cape Horn (42 days, 2 hours, 52 seconds) and we were four and a half days ahead *Sport Elec's* time, but to me a Cape Horn rounding was another step on my quest to a Vendée entry. I secretly hoped that the next time I saw the Cape I would be alone, aboard my own boat.

No sooner had we turned the corner and headed for the Straits of Le Maire than the clouds lifted and the sun came out. It was as if someone had flicked a switch. We celebrated with a great lunch and a splash of Burgundy, and watched the snow-capped mountains of southern Chile pass by. The water was smooth and we were back up to full main and gennaker. The Southern Ocean was behind us. For the first time since the start our bows were pointed due north not for weather reasons but on a course for home.

▶ 42 days, 2 hours, 52 seconds later we finally reach the summit... Cape Horn

Photo: © Jean-Baptiste Epron

CHAPTER 9

'Today I have the task of revealing damage which has been the source of great concern for several days now. If the ball breaks the mast will come down. It's as simple and dangerous as that.'

Log 21

Damage is something that we think about all the time. We are on the home stretch in an ocean riddled with debris.

In my mind there were six stages to our journey; the start to the Equator, the Equator to the Cape of Good Hope, Cape of Good Hope to Australia and the halfway mark, Australia to Cape Horn, Cape Horn to the Equator (crossing our outward track) and finally the Equator to the finish line. With Cape Horn behind us we were entering the last stages of the voyage. Two-thirds of the planet was behind us, but a lot of sailing still lay ahead.

Cape Horn to the Equator was the part of the voyage that we had all been dreading. When we sailed south to the Southern Ocean we had sailed down the west side of the South Atlantic high with a fair wind from behind. We would now have to sail back up that way with that wind on the nose. By now it was no secret that *Orange* did not like sailing to windward and we were about to start one of the longest windward beats of our lives.

I thought back to the Whitbread and spending several days crashing through steep aggressive seas. I also reflected on the actual damage that Club Med suffered in this region. Off the coast of Argentina they were nailed by a severe front that whipped up a choppy sea. Pounding into it one of the crew noticed that paint on the port hull had chipped. Chipping paint meant that something was moving and further investigation inside the hull revealed a serious problem: the inner core had come loose from the outer skins. If the problem had spread the integrity of the hull would have been in question. The crew set about fixing the area with plates through-bolted in much the same way as Yves and Pépêche had repaired the aft beam on *Orange*. From there on the boat had to be nursed home. You can't win if you don't finish. Club Med had a race to win; we had a record to break.

 *See Log 21*

I moved into my own bunk, a space onboard that was not being used, probably because of its size, or lack there of. Until now I had been swapping with Hervé as he and I were on different watches. From the Horn to the finish we restructured the watches to take advantage of the rapidly changing conditions. Now Hervé and I would be off watch at the same time. My new bunk was below his. The gap between the two was such that I could not turn on my side or roll over but on the other hand it was easy to elbow him in the ribs when his snoring got too loud. The lack of area didn't faze me – it was good to have my own space which was dry and comfortable. I even put up a few photos, and made a little pouch for my music disks, note pad and torch so I could write my journals. In my notebook I wrote lists and designs for my dream boat. On the cover I had

a list of people to think of and thank every day, like a child saying his prayers before going to sleep. On that list were the names of every member of our shore team that had worked so hard for us.

For now the wind remained from behind and we gybed our way to the Falkland Islands. Almost immediately it started to get warmer and we were able to enjoy sitting on deck rather than huddling in the cuddy. We knocked off a day's run of 536 miles/862 kilometres one day and just over 500 miles/805 kilometres the next. Suddenly the Falkland Islands were right in front of us. Bruno described the situation in his morning chat:

We have decided to gybe. Otherwise we will be making an assault on the cliffs of the Falkland Islands. We are currently 15 miles from Port Stanley and Cape Pembroke.

We never actually saw the Falklands which was a little disappointing. Our only sightings of land had been Madeira in the first few days after the start then Cape Horn – both lasting just a few hours. We actually diverted a little closer to Madeira than originally planned to drop off a pigeon that had hitched a ride. Vlad ran around catching the bird and repeatedly throwing it into the air towards Madeira, only to have it circle the boat

▲ Heading north into calmer waters?

145

▲ Yves and J-B on the grinder

and land back on deck like a boomerang. This happened several times before it finally saw the island and headed off to shore.

We gybed to pass to the west of the Falklands and thought about how best to position ourselves for the weather ahead. Another complicated weather pattern was developing: there was an intense low-pressure system off the coast of Argentina and it was making its way in our direction. The South Atlantic High was well formed to the east of us and we were looking to thread our way between the two. The problem was that, once again, the weather charts did not agree with each other. Bruno and Gilles were pulling weather information from both American and European sources, and while both models agreed on the weather for the next 36 hours, they did not agree at all after that. As Bruno said:

The situation is definitely not simple. We are going to have to aim for a mousehole. It's a race against the clock and that's why we are driving hard at the moment.

And we were still driving hard downwind under spinnaker. The waves off the leeward hull were hissing past like the carving spray from a slalom skier. After more than 20,000 miles/32,000 kilometres of sailing it was still a thrill to watch the water rip past the boat. *Orange* was eating up the miles as we made easterly ground to avoid the approaching front. I wondered if it was worth sailing that extra distance to avoid a fast moving storm or if we should just sail as close as possible to the best course home and deal with what came our way. Over the next few days we sailed from the longitude of 67° W at Cape Horn to 33° W, which was half the easterly ground needed to reach the finish line.

One morning Jo-Jo was carefully preparing himself a cocktail of porridge, milk, sugar and raisins in preparation for his watch. He was just about ready to tuck in and enjoy it when the helmsman planted the bows and the whole thing went flying. It exploded all over the galley, followed by a torrent of common Australian expressions that I had exchanged for French ones throughout the last 47 days at sea.

It's pretty wild sailing this boat in dodgy conditions. You creep your bows closer to the wind to increase speed then, boom, you are hit by a big gust or are picked up by a large wave and you are just off! The speed increase is amazing. Anyone standing falls on their butts, sometimes even the helmsman. Everybody braces for the sudden punch into the wave in front and a solid wall of water to engulf the cockpit.

 *See Log 22*

Gilles summed up his approach to hygiene during the morning chat:

I promised to take a shower as soon as we arrived in the Atlantic but I have not kept my promise. It's still too cold and the weather situation we're having is not simple.

He and Bruno continued to analyse the weather maps trying to figure out the best way up the Atlantic. In the end it became obvious that we could not keep going east. We were managing to outrun the low pressure but we were also running up against the high and the wind was starting to drop. Finally Bruno called for a gybe to the north. It was a tough call because the new course was directly towards the system we had been trying to outrun, and the front was packing a steady 45 knots of wind. Despite the grim forecast many of the guys were happy to be heading north again. North was in the direction of home and we were keen to get there.

Log 22

Last night whilst getting ready for our watch, the lads on deck were complaining about the cold so I donned an extra layer. We were sailing with one reef in the main and the spinnaker with the true wind speed ranging from 16 to 38 knots. Big, big waves sending you hurtling off at 35 knots of boat speed into black pits. Everybody is braced down below as we have already made a few minor stuffs. It's a little chaotic on the helm and I walked away from my driving spell covered in sweat. So much for it being cold. Everybody is monitoring the sea temperature and holding out to see what becomes of this storm to the north of us before attempting to catch up on a bit of hygiene maintenance. Most of us are still in the same set of thermal underwear that we have been in for the past 15 days or so. We only have one clean pair left and do not wish to take the risk of getting them wet during the oncoming strong winds. I have not shaven for about two weeks as it's better to have a beard protecting your skin when you are wrapped in Gore-Tex with your collar fastened tight around your face. We wash with baby wipes regularly but I am looking forward to my first real bucket bath when the sea temperature gets warmer, which is, unfortunately, still about five days away. Nice thought!

Log 23

It's an anxious period
awaiting a storm. We all
know the procedure but
whilst your heart is saying
'you're almost there' the
chance of breakage due to
high winds and rough seas
makes you feel like the
finish is another three
months away.
We kept looking to the west
to see if there was any
change, but it was all
clear. We were sailing with
a full mainsail and solent,
and the moderate seas were
helping the boat speed. In
the early evening we noticed
some frontal clouds rolling
in and we spent the night
skirting the edge of them.
It was pitch black out and
the mast was beginning to
hum with the increase in
wind. We crossed 40º S and
officially left the Roaring
40s behind.
Yesterday was our first real
day in about 20 days that we
had clear skies and
sunshine. I sat, for a
period, under the companion
way dome and absorbed some
of the sun's natural warmth
through the Perspex.
 Now the storm is clawing
over us and the night is
pitch black.

See Log 23

By morning the sky was overcast and grey, and the squalls were coming one after the other. The wind was right on the nose, as forecast, and the seas began to get lumpy. After the last few days of wonderful sailing it was grim to be back in this foul weather dealing with an approaching gale, but there was nothing we could do but to hang on and punch through it. The wind increased to 42 knots and we reefed and set the small staysail. The rain started to lash down, drenching everything, but also washing away the salt that had accumulated on the deck and rigging. We huddled in the cuddy bracing with each slam as *Orange* continued to make good northing.

Out of nowhere two albatrosses cruised by, looking at us with their dark, knowing eyes and then they swooped away gracefully and headed back south to colder latitudes. It was strange to see them so far north. Moments later we saw flying fish. Again it was unusual to see these two creatures of different seas so close to each other – almost as if one was waving us goodbye and the other saying hello.

We broke free of the low, shook out the reefs and set a larger headsail. The conditions quickly became very pleasant as we had made good miles to the north during our period of bashing and crashing. The water was now warming. I was a little concerned that we were still too far to the east for crossing the Doldrums, but only time would tell. The Equator was still 2,000 miles/3,220 kilometres away. Yann Eliès summed up life on board in his log:

We're beginning to take it easier with the improving climate. The boat and the clothes are drying out. We're in excellent shape, the meals are perfectly balanced and we have no skin problems to complain about any more, which for sailors who have spent an extended time in the damp on these boats is quite remarkable.

My log read:

Just got rid of the beard and had a tub. Feeling a lot better, am ready for the nightclub but instead have four hours helming and trimming ahead.

We took advantage of the fine weather to air the boat out and dry things. Sébastien Josse took apart the watermaker which had been giving out brackish water for the past few days. The boat looked like a laundry with all the washing strewn everywhere but with every mile we sailed north life on board got a little better. We really appreciated small things like a

little sunshine, being able to use the toilet comfortably, and crossing the trampoline without getting soaked. The water turned a brilliant turquoise and there were flying fish everywhere; we were definitely entering the tropics.

We had been at sea for 50 days and logged almost 22,000 miles/35,400 kilometres. The statistics from Mer et Media told us that we had approximately 3,840 miles/6,180 kilometres to go to the finish line and we had 21 days in which to do it if we were going to beat *Sport Elec's* time. Their calculations spat out the magic number: to beat the record we would have to average about 7.61 knots. The cat was more than able to average that speed – we could easily double it. But there were hidden dangers ahead: a submerged log washed down from the Amazon, or what if we hit a whale? What if the rig came down or even the mainsail came apart? What if there was some damage to the boat that we had overlooked and it caused us to slow down? The numbers were interesting but we were not counting our chickens. The sea is the master. The Doldrums lay ahead and then there was the whole length of the North Atlantic to tackle.

We saw a cargo ship. Gilles called them up on the radio for a chat and discovered that they were on passage from Singapore to Buenos Aires. They had probably left Singapore before we left Brest. This was the first vessel that we had seen since a fishing boat south of South Africa.

Our early easting seemed to be paying dividends; we were well positioned for our approach to the Doldrums. Whether they planned it that way or not, Bruno and Gilles took credit for our placing:

As soon as we rounded the Horn, we had to take a long term view because ahead of us the situation looked hopeless. Taking the direct route, that's to say the one usually taken by sailors up the South American coast, would be taking big risks for the boat without the certitude of consequential gains on the scorecard. We are happy to have entered the trades without breaking anything. Trades that are already allowing us to concentrate on crossing the Equator. The boat is nice and dry, very sound and in good shape. The temperatures are mild and the flying fish are back.

Our captain seemed pleased with life and he deserved to be. He had plotted a good course through the southern latitudes, pushing the boat when we needed to make up miles and the conditions allowed, and holding back when the seas were too rough to sail safely or there was a chance of damaging the boat. I admired his sense of balance. His vast experience of multihulls and years spent at sea on all sorts of other craft had given him an innate sense of when to go fast and when to sail safe. We were all learning a lot from him.

▲ Bruno checking in with the boys

Photo: © Jean-Baptiste Epron

After the long slog across the Southern Ocean it was nice to be able to do a night watch with your shirt off, feeling the warm wind blowing on your skin. The tropics were being kind to us; I knew that once we were back in the northern hemisphere the days would be getting colder again, so I really appreciated every hour of this pleasant sailing. One morning I took a little time out, grabbed my mini-disk player and headed for the bowsprit where I sat watching the waves pass under me. The water was a fabulous colour and *Orange* was really cruising along.

Looking aft I was again impressed by the size of the boat. The vast expanse of trampoline seemed to stretch out forever. It was suspended between the two razor-thin hulls. The mast towered above with hundreds of square metres of fabric, sailcloth that had caught the wind and propelled us almost all the way around the world. The second of my life goals was well on the way to becoming a reality. I wondered about the third. A solo spin around the planet, the whole way, alone? A daunting thought.

The road from that room in the New Zealand Maritime Museum, where I first laid eyes on the Trophée Jules Verne in 1995, to the turquoise blue ocean that I was now sailing on had been long but incredibly interesting. I simply went to work. I sailed and sailed and then I sailed some more. I travelled and lived out of a backpack. I struggled and soared, sometimes both on the same day. I slept on the docks in a steel ship's container because I couldn't afford a bed. I bought a copy of *ENZA's* video and I cannot count how many times I watched it. In Australia I set up my bike on a stationary trainer and pushed out the miles, in my living room. I set a high tempo and would not back off until the lads had rounded Cape Horn. I would then wind down through to the finish. I can still picture the crew's faces, the elation. I can still hear their voices. I wondered if we would experience such contentment? We had 22 days to keep our world together, to avoid damage, to preserve ourselves and each other; 22 days to sail a further 5,000 miles/8,046 kilometres; only then would we know. I mentioned on the website how I had been inspired and driven by the admiration I had for my heroes on *Commodore Explorer*, *Sport Elec* and *ENZA*. When Angus Buchanan from the crew of *ENZA* wrote back, I was blown away.

◀ Time out – taking in the scenery from the bow sprit, comtemplating life!

But suddenly, all this introspection was interrupted. At the base of the huge wing mast is a titanium ball. It is about 5 inches/12 centimetres in diameter and it takes the full load of the mast, rigging and sails, whilst allowing the mast to rotate. The compression on the ball is over 60 tonnes. Ronan, our rigger, was the first to notice that something was wrong. Strange squeaking noises were heard coming from the ball each time the mast bent or turned. On closer inspection he noticed a crack, a crack that went almost all the way around. If the ball broke in half the mast would come down: the rig would punch through the mid-beam or skip off the base, tear through the trampoline before plunging into the sea. Everything abve the boom would crash across the decks. The rigging would go slack, and the mast would crash over the side. It was a perilous situation. For days we worried. Only those directly connected to the problem were initially informed: our team, our design engineers and the relevant rescue services. When Bruno felt the time was right, he made a release to the public:

Today I have the task of revealing damage which has been the source of great concern for several days now. If the ball breaks the mast will come down. It's as simple and as dangerous as that.

Almost instantly our world went from carefree to very tenuous. If the mast came down we would be in serious trouble, not only from a record point of view, but a safety one as well. We were pretty well in the middle of nowhere; the nearest reference point was the Equator – not a lot of use. All of us had vivid memories of the mast breaking after our first start – if the mast came down now it would be far more catastrophic. Our options were few and none of them particularly great. Firstly, we could stop racing and head for the nearest port. Or, secondly – Bruno got on the phone to Yann Penfornis, the boat's architect and builder in France, and between them they came up with a plan for reinforcing the ball.

The skilled boatbuilders onboard would make a carbon collar to wrap around the ball. It would not add much to the reinforcement of the ball itself; titanium is incredibly strong and even wrapping it in carbon would be of little help, but the collar would sit around the ball helping to maintain its location if it separated completely. If we could immobilise the mast and keep the rigging taught there was less chance of it coming down. Yves le Blévec set about making the collar and he described what he did in the daily chat:

Together with Yann Penfornis at Multiplast we have created a coupling to support the ball just in case the part gives out. We have had to wait until the boat was sliding along nice and dry in the

▲ The ball joint at the base of the mast

▲ Yves at work again

▲ The repair

Photos: © Jean-Baptiste Epron

tradewinds before being able to build and position this clamp at the mast's base.

As Yves and his helpers set up shop below to build the critical part, the rest of us tried to figure out the best way to baby the mast. Initially we reduced sail but we soon found that with a reef in the main the mast moved around a lot more than it did with full main, so we decided to keep the pressure on with full sail. Bruno and Gilles studied the weather maps and concluded that we would have to sail a different course back to France. We would have to make a big swing into the North Atlantic to avoid some strong low-pressure systems near the African coast. The detour would take us longer than anticipated, but we all agreed that, if we made it, it would have been well worth the extra miles sailed. My log at the time described the situation and shows some of the stress we were under:

 *See Log 24*

While we sat and talked about our options, and discussed a strategy for the rest of the voyage, the weather gods treated us to a magnificent display of nature's beauty. The sky was a mixture of black rainsqualls, blue sky, white cumulus clouds, orange and red sunrays and even a rainbow for a period. It looked like an artist had seriously overdone it. While we sat mesmerised by the sight, *Orange* romped silently into the northern hemisphere. I had just crossed the Equator for the seventh time under sail.

Log 24

I trust everyone understands why we held off information about our mast problem. I think we all needed to deal with the situation onboard before we became overwhelmed with advice. So the basics are: the mast is stepped on a ball joint very similar to a tow ball on your car. This allows the wing mast to rotate. The ball has a crack around half of its perimeter. Quite serious. For several days the mast has been making the most horrendous noise as our bows slap over the waves. Yves has made an effort to retain the ball in the event that it shears off completely by laminating carbon fibre around the base, plate and beam. Whether or not it will be enough is impossible to say.

There is not much we can do now other than to just keep sailing smart. Try to preserve when we can. The consequences of total failure are daunting, but we knew that risk level when we signed on. I believe we are in no more danger than any other day onboard these beasts. I think it's the thought of the 1.8 tonne mast, 38 metres long, with over 800 square metres of sail, tumbling down around you that has put us all on edge. At least we are aware and know where the danger zones are onboard.

I have been able to push it out of my mind for long periods. If it happens, it happens. We can no longer monitor the crack as it's wrapped in carbon and out of view. Either it stays standing or we have issues. Big issues. We are prepared in regard to safety equipment so we shall see.

Photo: © Jean-Baptiste Epron

'The final 10 miles/16 kilometres were counted down out loud. Inside our final mile we were all yelling out the decreasing numbers at the top of our voices: Trois... Deux... Un... FINI!'

Log 25

I cannot stop feeling that
if we don't succeed then the
whole experience will have
been a total waste of time.
I know that this is not the
case in reality but I feel
it and it's strong.

J-B had brought with him a blow-up plastic globe that spent most of the trip bouncing around inside the port hull. He updated our position on it regularly with a thick black marker pen. It reminded me how much it had meant to sail the Whitbread – the whole way around the world. It leaves you with a special feeling.

New press releases were sent out announcing our arrival back in the northern hemisphere, but to us they were just bits of paper. The real story to us was the 38-metre mast towering above the boat, and the small titanium ball supporting it all. If the ball broke, down would come the mast along with all our hopes and dreams. That was the reality. We had come a long, long way, but there was still even further to go to successfully complete our circumnavigation.

It had taken us 11 days, 1 hour and 57 minutes to sail from Cape Horn to the Equator. It was a new record from Ushant to the second crossing of the Equator. That time stood at 53 days, 4 hours and 49 minutes. It was hard to believe that we had almost sailed all the way around the world in just over seven weeks. We had already crossed our outbound track so in some sense we had completed a circumnavigation, but the Jules Verne rules are clear: in order to set a record you need to start from a point above 48 degrees 30 minutes north and finish above 48 degrees 30 minutes north. We had 17 days to sail the last approximately 2,460 miles/3,960 kilometres to the finish, and we had to average just 6.02 knots to do so. It was now a question of luck, and our skills as crew. We were a well-honed team by now but we knew that it was important to be very careful in everything we did and to not let down our guard.

See Log 25

I sat with Bruno at the chart table and we discussed his plan of attack for the North Atlantic. Bruno was clear in his intention. He did not want to smash the record. He would be happy to simply better the record and we all agreed. Now was the time for some very serious sailing. We would baby the boat, sail judiciously, and if we were lucky that beautiful trophy would be ours. In the daily chat Bruno summed up the strategy for the leg to the finish:

We have no options to try because we must fetch the leading winds where they are. We're going to do a big loop to the west hoping that we can sail with beam winds in the trades, then pick up the leading winds that are turning around the high.

This big loop would add approximately 25 per cent to the length of the last leg of our voyage.

▲ J-B's plastic globe

Photo: © Jean-Baptiste Epron

▶ Altering course in a desperate bid simply to finish

CHASING the DAWN

Log 26

This is brutal! Patience? If
I hear that word again, I'll
scream! Ah... hang on, our
display unit that is now
permanently fixed on our
latitude has just clicked
over to 7° N. Now that makes
us feel better!

We still had the Doldrums to cross and the winds were very light. The day after we crossed the Equator we only managed to sail 268 miles/430 kilometres. Bruno said on the daily chat:

Fortunately the sea has calmed down since yesterday evening and there is a fair bit of light wind ahead. Patience is of the essence. On a course like this you can find yourself flying down waves in the Southern Ocean at 30 knots and climbing up the Atlantic at just 8 knots. Every sailor knows that light wind is often harder than heavy weather. You have to be that much more attentive and concentrate all the more in light winds where every mile clocked up is worth two or three what it would be otherwise.

 *See Log 26*

Hervé Jan came out with the quote of the tour:

It's a bit like eternity. It's good for a while but it gets a bit long towards the end.

The on-watch team were doing everything they could to squeeze an extra tenth of a knot from the boat. We were trimming sails to each puff of wind or change in direction, concentrating and working hard. The weather was distinctly summery; the skies clear, the winds light and there was the unmistakable smell of sunscreen in the air. With not a lot to think about my mind wandered back to the days hanging out at Sailboard Headquarters in Sandringham waiting for the afternoon sea breeze to set up for a great windsurfing session at Ricketts Point. It seemed like a long time ago.

Another maxi-cat was also at sea in this ocean in search of a record. The crew of *Maiden 2*, ex-Club Med, was attempting the Cadiz–San Salvador or Route of Discovery record; a fast tradewinds Atlantic record. We had been following their progress as many great friends were onboard including two crew members from the *EDS Atlantic Challenge* onboard *Kingfisher*. They were also dreaming of the Jules Verne and this was part of their build-up and training. Unfortunately after getting so close we received the news that day that they had abandoned the attempt as the time limit had expired.

On *Orange* we knew that the time was cast in stone. *Sport Elec* had finished and had established the existing record. I looked up from my daydreaming and the ocean was still a large, blue marble and our giant cat was loping across its surface. The massive sails cast a long, cool shadow on the water where Portuguese men-of-war floated past, their bright purple adding another hue to an already colourful setting. I felt

pretty sure that we were going to set a new record. Everything felt right about it. The mast was holding, the crew were amazing, the boat was in good shape and we were ready to become record breakers.

We picked up the tradewinds and left the Inter-Tropic Convergence Zone behind for good. Orange picked up the fresh winds and took off as if sensing the excitement we all felt on board. We had eaten our way through most of the supplies and burned most of the fuel, and as a result the boat felt very different from when we sailed south. On the daily chat Bruno said:

The behaviour of the boat has become very pleasant. Orange *is very sound. She picks up very quickly and the helmsman can really play the waves.*

We were heading towards a point west of the Azores. Bruno and Gilles were working to find favourable winds that did not over-tax the boat. High pressure dominated the area ahead of us and we were looking to hook onto the southwesterly flow across the top of it. If they got it right, the wind would slingshot us to the finish. Gilles said:

We are probably gong to have to gybe downwind. The North Atlantic lows are there waiting for us and they will take us all the way to the finish line.

I was starting to lose confidence that we would finish on my birthday, but I had spent one birthday at sea before. In 1998 during Leg 8 of the Whitbread I turned 30 and we won the leg. The guys were really enjoying the final push and were up to their usual practical jokes. Benoit crept out of the darkness and scared the life out of me by bursting through the waterproof screen that protected the media suite. I was writing my log, concentrating on putting my fingers on the right keys, when he jumped out at me. Ahhh! I wondered if he was the one who had left the dead flying fish in the companionway right where I would step on it in bare feet.

As we sailed gracefully across the vast sea we noticed a tinge of red covering the yacht – it was dust from a far away Saharan sandstorm settling on the boat. It coated the mast, sails and rigging leaving everything looking like it was rusting away. On 28 April, our 58th day at sea we opened our last weekly bag of 'sundry items': ketchup, toilet paper, etc, and began rationing food.

As the calendar flipped over to May we celebrated our 60th day at sea. I was on deck tending the jib sheet. The winds were steady and there was not much to do so I was in half a daze. Hervé was driving when I noticed him frantically turning the wheel. He just kept winding it, but nothing happened. He did not say anything and I was looking out of the

◄ We can do this

167

corner of my eye wondering what he was doing, when he suddenly started calling out to the other guys in French. Then he said to me, 'I think you'd better grab the other wheel.' I ran across the trampoline and grabbed the port steering wheel bringing the boat back on course again. The steering cables had snapped, but having two wheels saved the day. OK, I am wide awake now.

With less than 2,000 miles/3,200 kilometres to go we were starting to get very excited. The press were demanding an ETA, but Bruno, not one to tempt fate, was being cagey: 'It depends on a lot of things.' Thoughts of the finish automatically turned to thoughts of life on land and Jean-Baptiste Epron spoke for all of us when he was asked about finishing on the daily chat:

It's true that we're torn between enjoying it a bit longer and finishing. But I think that a walk in the country, in the woods with the birds singing would also be quite nice.

The seas were being kind to us and *Orange* was slicing through the water at full speed. We had long since lost any perspective on how fast we were travelling. To us 30 knots and 500-mile/800-kilometre days were normal. I was starting to think seriously about how it was going to be back on dry land and was expecting it to be a difficult transition. After the Whitbread Race I deliberately maintained my watch system for a while, waking during the night and walking around the house. I remember one night in particular when I was woken by a storm. I got out of bed, rugged up and went outside. I sat among the trees which were swaying wildly in the dark with wind whistling through the branches. I couldn't help thinking that someone would be experiencing the same storm out on a remote sea. Where was my boat? Where was my team?

There is a minor downside to sailing around the world so fast and that is knowing that you have missed so many sights along the way. We didn't even see a lot of sea life. I remember on my first race around the world we would sometimes see five whales in one day. This time I only saw three the entire trip and one was dead. We did see a lot of birds; I have never before seen so many albatrosses. If they really are the souls of lost sailors, as old maritime lore would have it, then I think they all wanted to go for a ride on our orange machine.

We skirted the Azores, 500 miles/800 kilometres to the west. The westernmost island is called Flores, meaning flowers. Had we been closer we would have enjoyed the smell of land but it was not to be. Still, we were getting more and more signs of civilisation, as Gilles described in his log:

This morning we were on a collision course with a yacht. The boat is sliding along perfectly, with full mainsail and gennaker in 10 to 12 knots of wind. We will soon be able to luff and head for Brest.

We started to see more sea life. There were dolphins and a whale breached in the distance. The waters around the Azores were still a hunting ground for whales two decades ago, but since that has stopped we were able to enjoy one of the most spectacular sights a sailor can see.

Bruno was still being pestered by the press to come up with an ETA:

It's still difficult to predict. If we average 18 knots we will cross the line at midday on Sunday. At 17 knots it will be Sunday evening, but of course Orange *can also go faster.*

I was starting to feel like a child waiting for Christmas, we were getting that close. At least I was able to keep my head together unlike J-B who woke for his watch and proceeded to get his whole team out of bed and on deck, only to realise that they were all an hour early! The mast was not making grinding noises anymore and we took this to be a good sign. Then we received the news that *Amer Sports Two* in the Volvo Ocean race had been dismasted northwest of our position in strong winds, and the fine line between victory and disaster loomed again. It's not over till it's over. We still had 1,000 miles/1,600 kilometres to go.

While we were watching every click of the GPS, the PR machine on land was getting into full swing. People from all over the world were following our progress and hanging on every written word. Even the Australian Embassy in Paris and the Australian High Commission in London were getting my daily emails and reading them with interest. If we broke the record we would be only the fourth successful attempt in eleven tries, *Commodore Explorer*, *ENZA* and *Sport Elec* being the other three. We could become members of a very exclusive club.

There is no denying that we were anxious. I even caught myself out one morning, just after a nap. I was feeling slightly frustrated about the lack of speed; our average over the previous hour had dropped to 18 knots. After splashing cold water on my face and wiping the sleep from my eyes, it occurred to me that most sailors would never experience sailing at 18 knots in their entire lives. I had momentarily lost a sense of perspective and appreciation of just how fast we were really going. We had been averaging over 18 knots since the start.

'It does one good to see the GPS with three figures now with under 1,000 miles to go,' Sebastian told those listening to the daily chat, and indeed it did. We were not free and clear just yet though. The weather model showed a glitch some 80 miles/130 kilometres from the finish. Bruno commented:

▲ J-B waking the lads for a watch

There is a small problem between us and the finish but it's not really a problem. Our rhythm of life remains very constant. There is no haste, no impatience. Everybody remains focused and at the same time there is a sort of detachment. There are mixed feelings between serenity and an urge to be back.

I was having a hard time sleeping and kept pacing the boat, checking the chart and looking at the weather maps. Then a strange thing happened. I received an email from my mum and dad and it was in French. French! They don't speak a word of French. I was mystified, but happy nonetheless.

On 4 May we were just over 300 miles/482 kilometres from the finish. It was starting to look like we might finish on my birthday after all. Gilles said:

We are just 328 miles/528 kilometres from joy. Only one small low pressure to deal with and then we are home. Home. There is no impatience on board. Just pleasure. It looks like we will be arriving on Nick Moloney's birthday and since there is no cake on board we will be giving him our Australian flag.

For most of the tour, three flags flapped off our stern; the French flag, the Breton flag and the Australian flag. For this I was flattered until I discovered that its relevance had something to do with a burial at sea.

In the early afternoon we were still making excellent speed and it seemed as if nothing could go wrong. The water hissed past the hulls as our big, beautiful yacht ate up the last few miles. We had a full main and large gennaker set and we were spitting out miles at a rate of some 25 knots (40 kilometres) an hour. I was down below in the media centre composing an email when I felt the boat load up rapidly. I could see the steering cables as the helmsman was trying to bear off. I jumped to my feet as the load kept coming on, not sure if we were flying a hull with the big gennaker or not, but it sure felt like it. I started running down the aisle to the main hatch. 'Someone ease something,' I yelled from down below. All the guys off watch were piling out of their bunks and grabbing wet weather gear. I was sure that we were going to flip, then all of a sudden, BANG! The load immediately subsided. It had to be the mast, nothing else could make such a noise. My heart was in my mouth. I had seen this movie before.

I bolted on deck and immediately looked aloft. The mast was still there, but the gennaker was flapping wildly and the guys were running everywhere with stunned looks on their faces. We were still not sure what had happened. Then Florent pointed to a broken line. He had been easing the sheet to take the load off the gennaker to avoid a capsize when the

sheet suddenly snapped. We recovered quickly and were back sailing again, but the thought that was on all our minds was what might have happened had the line not broken? It was too much to contemplate. So close yet so far. It was shocking to think just how close we have come to total disaster – we all breathed a hugh sigh of relief. Shortly after the incident with the gennaker the wind started to die and we ghosted through the night.

Our last heart-stopper came that night. I had just handed the wheel over to Hervé. We were sailing in great steady winds, quite pressured up with the medium gennaker when suddenly with a loud roar the gennaker tore into three pieces. I remember thinking, bloody hell, this is never ending! Had we let down our guard now that we were almost home? We all ran onto the front tramp and wrestled the bits to the deck as we had done with the same sail when the mast had failed on our first attempt at leaving. We changed sails to a much smaller headsail, leaving us underpowered, but it gave us time to calm down. We simply had to get there and we now needed no more reminders. Our nerves were shot.

▲ Hoisting small headsail after breaking gennaker... our nerves were shot

This was to be our last night at sea and none of us slept. Thoughts of land filled every moment; we sat around and talked about the trip and about what we were going to do once we crossed the line. We had waited so long for this night and now we were nearly there. It was even more poignant after the stress of the last few days with the cracked ball and the action that day but even the mast was quiet.

Bruno wrote in his log:

I'm beginning to feel a touch of nostalgia when I look at this narrow tube of carbon in which 13 men have lived in perfect harmony for 64 days.

Mer et Media continued:

Orange is aiming to cross the line in the immediate vicinity of the old Ushant lighthouse where the judges of the World Sailing Speed Council will be posted to immortalise the end of the adventure.

▲ Discussion and reflection: tomorrow we will be with family and friends

I sat and wrote an email trying to put into words how I felt and to thank everyone, but the words still seem inadequate:

We are 200 miles/320 kilometres from the finish and that's awesome. I am an incredibly lucky person and nobody knows this more than me. There is an amazing team in an office on the Isle of Wight headed by Helen King and Josie Robinson that have been updating the website and keeping people informed of our progress. There is also a crew on a barge in Paris. Cheers guys and girls, you are incredible. Mark and Ellen are working hard on Kingfisher and securing sponsorship for my next big race which will be solo race across the Atlantic from St Malo, my surrogate home in France, to the island of Guadeloupe in the French Caribbean. The race is called the Route du Rhum and will be my first step towards my third offshore sailing goal. To circumnavigate this globe once more but alone. Through these people's efforts the opportunity is created for me to do what I really love doing. It's been tough being the only non-Frenchman on board, but every time I got down I leant on a simple life perspective that every long distance sailor has learnt to live by and only comes from experience. I am forever in debt to Bruno, Orange and the team for allowing and accepting me on board this amazing journey. Thanks everyone onshore for your uplifting emails – this has been my greatest treat and the single thing I have looked forward to the most throughout this voyage. Finally, thanks Flavie for being my connection to earth for the past 64 days.

During the last 100 miles/160 kilometres the wind began to build from a favourable direction. Throughout the night we began tentatively to believe. On the that last evening I was congratulated by the crew for surviving 34 years on the planet. It was my birthday and the race against the Jules Verne record had developed another link: get Moloney home for his birthday!

I took aside Hervé, Yann Eliès and Ronan individually, the guys that I had spent most time on deck with since Cape Horn, and thanked them for making such an incredible memory. Our last dawn broke and we were all simply buzzing.

▶ Overleaf... The 13 fastest sailors in the world!

The saddest part about re-living this journey through writing this book is that my memories and emotions will never be quite as sharp as they were on that magical day. That's life, but my heart is pounding hard as I type this. I can vividly recall being below deck, about 50 miles/80 kilometres from the finish, when I heard the beating of a low flying chopper over our heads. We all ran on deck and there it was hovering within metres of the stern. Hanging out of the side door were the first and last faces that we had seen throughout our 64 days at sea other than the 13 of us onboard, making me think of everyone awaiting our arrival in Brest. They were as elated as we were. Gilles Martin Raget clicked away with his camera and the crew grouped together, the fastest sailors around the world. We stood together forming a band of memories and friendship, solidarity that stretched across the back beam. Still charging along at 30 knots we stood proud, together, 13 men and one amazing craft. So many miles astern, so few ahead; so many memories, amazing images, some peaceful and beautiful, some horrific and ugly. Each of us had our own bank. As we posed for the cameras I could feel the strength of the embrace from those on either side. Shoulder to shoulder, side by side we were living the dream.

At 30 knots, 50 miles/80 kilometres evaporates very quickly and before we knew it we could see the finish. We gathered on the port side of *Orange* and watched the miles drop away as information from our onboard GPS relayed data to the on-deck displays. The final 10 miles/16 kilometres were counted down out loud. Inside our final mile we were all yelling out the decreasing numbers at the top of our voices: Trois... Deux... Un... FINI!

We all began yelling and embracing like players in a solid contact rugby team, falling about the tramp, tackling each other, embracing, slapping backs and palms. We completely lost it! We yelled, we laughed, our eyes even welled, we stared momentarily at each other with thanks and admiration. Even today these emotions are strong and powerful.

Fresh food came onboard along with an array of journalists, including one who was interviewing us live on French national radio. It was mayhem. I was simply stoked to see new faces. It was strange to see these people, frightened of our world, jumping every time the boat let out a creak or groan. It occurred to me just how confident and fluent we had become with the sea, the enormous tensions and our bright orange maxi-cat.

As we sailed up the channel surrounded by the flotilla of welcoming craft packed with people yelling and cheering, we were all busy with journalists giving a brief on the last two months at sea. None of us could help but be preoccupied with our own search amongst the boats that had ventured out to meet us. Bruno kept us busy, showing off to the crowd, reefs in and out, hull flying. We were having a fantastic time – but all the time we were searching for familiar faces.

The first friend I saw was Helen King, She was on a packed sponsor boat with James Blanshard who had come down from Paris to represent the Australian Embassy. Hels was there waving away. This was a really magical connection. Hels had been so connected to this trip and, along with Josie, had been bringing all the news to the readers of our website. I knew how hard they had worked throughout the winter – they had hardly seen the light of day. They arrived at their cave-like office in Cowes on the Isle of Wight in darkness and long before they left in the evening the sun had been and gone. They live every moment of The Offshore Challenges Team Ventures through Ellen and myself.

The next person I saw was Mark Turner, my manager and sailing team mate. He gave me the wave that has now become a custom: a cross between a wave and salute. – he's happy and it shows.

I am looking for Flav, my girl. I cannot wait to see her. Her parents had come down from the north of France to welcome me back, I was very flattered by this as I knew that most of the crew being French would have family at the finish. My family lives in Australia but there was a slight chance that Dad might be in the UK on business and able to make the dash to Brest for our arrival but I didn't want to get my hopes up.

It wasn't until we stopped outside the harbour to take down the sails for the last time that I caught a glimpse of an Australian Flag on an Orange support boat on our starboard side. My eyes raced to focus. I could clearly see Flav waving wildly and dad hurling around the Aussie flag, both with huge grins, screaming and yelling. Suddenly Flav embraced a lady standing next to her and I realised it was Mum. Never in my thoughts or expectations would I have believed that she would be there. I could not believe my eyes. I was totally overcome, I couldn't speak, I could hardly breathe. I had never felt like this before. I began fighting back the tears, my head began to ache and I found myself losing it, with both hands on my head the tears streamed down my face. I fought hard to get it together. After several minutes dodging crew and cameras I found myself searching for things to do onboard, to get the boat ready for docking, just to fight off this overwhelming emotion. Whenever anyone came near me, all I could get out was a broken croaky, 'My mum's here!'

My mum is my biggest fan. She has put up with so much throughout my life. I have not been the easiest of children to raise, always dreaming and acting on my dreams. Some of my past antics have no doubt left her lying awake at night wondering if her boy is safe. With my professional arena being mostly in the northern hemisphere, my parents have often been a long way away. They were at the start and finish of the Whitbread which was an amazing experience for all of us. But then I go away again, In 2000 I began my quest towards this crazy speed record, non-stop sailing around the world. To be honest, mum was scared, when I left Australia after a brief visit, to return to Europe to make final preps to PlayStation for The Race, it was Mum's birthday and she was clearly frightened by these boats. I felt guilty and selfish. I drop everything and charge towards my goals, never stopping to think that people are genuinely concerned for my well-being. My sister struggles with this every day that I am at sea, weather it's training or racing.

As we began manoeuvring *Orange* into the basin at Brest the crowd control vessels formed a barrier to most spectator boats. Our families and friends headed for the dock to meet us as we came dockside. It seemed

▲ Yeah!

a painfully slow exercise but eventually we were once again tied to terra firma. Bruno's final words to us as his team were '*C'est bon, les gars!*' It was all over.

Orange had decided to restrict media access to the yacht and crews for an hour to allow us to spend some time with our loved ones before being mobbed by the press. As they were permitted onto the private dock, both Mum and Flav came running down the gangway with Dad a few metres behind. They scrambled over the lifelines around *Orange* and fell into my arms – another indescribable emotion that has my eyes welling with tears as I am typing this. The pride and, mostly, relief in my parents' faces was just too much. I thought of my whole family, my sister Peta, her husband Kimon, Shakira and Jamison (my niece and nephew), my childhood friends, my school friends, my brothers and sisters within the sailing fraternity, everyone who had given me a chance, taught me something new, those who had seen a light within and helped bring it out, those who had sacrificed so much to stand alongside and help all of us chase our dreams. What a moment.

When things began to calm down a little, I noticed Ellen MacArthur and the rest of the *Kingfisher* team on the dock amongst the crowd. I jumped off the cat and ran up the gangplank. People were grabbing me, screaming out in French, cheering and yelling but I was on emotional autopilot. The crowd control people picked up on where I wanted to go, formed a pathway and directed me through the maze of people and barricades to my *Kingfisher* team mates. Ellen appeared and just threw her arms around me like a wrestler. Within seconds the *Kingfisher* team and I were scrapping into a ball of interlocked arms cheering and yelling. It was my first physical contact with Mark and Helen as well. The choking emotional voice had been replaced with a stream of exclamations. That was awesome! I am so stoked!

An Australian flag that James had brought to Brest from the embassy in Paris was draped over me and as cameras rolled and clicked it began to sink in. We had made it! We had finally made it! We were the new Jules Verne record holders. 64 days, 8 hours, 37 minutes and 45 seconds had elapsed since the start; we had smashed more than seven days off the record. It was my 34th birthday. We had done it! My God, we had finally done it! Let the celebrations begin!

'Merci le bateau de nous avoir ramenés à la maison sains et saufs.'

Some may say that what we do is very selfish, expensive and not very productive, but what every adventurer does is make people believe. When we stepped our repaired mast in Vannes on the Brittany coast on that miserable rainy day, people wondered, some in their own minds, some out loud, what would become of these boys? Five hours later we threw away the lines that tied us to the Earth, in an act that was, to most, unheard of madness, and we began our quest for the second time. We knew that what we were about to attempt had a massive element of danger attached to it but we believed we could do it.

64 days, 8 hours, 37 minutes and 45 seconds later, two bright orange bows sailed back over the horizon with 13 beaming, weatherbeaten faces ready to tell the world where we had been and what we had done. On 5 May 2002 there was a mass of people on the water, on the docks and the foreshore, some of whom had doubted but now, in that special moment, I was surrounded by thousands of people who all believed that anything in life is possible. I like to think this is what I have contributed to this sometimes lost world. I have had the greatest job on the planet even if it's not strictly on Earth.

This book is dedicated to all those who wake up one memorable morning, climb out of a real bed, set the temperature of the shower how they want it... knowing that this is the last time they will have the opportunity to experience such everyday luxuries for around 60 days.

I am writing this in a hotel room in Paris on the eve of the opening of the 2002 Paris Boat Show. Almost seven months have passed since that incredible day in May. I am sad to say that I have not seen much of the team since leaving Brest. I guess we are all moving towards our next goals.

Bruno Peyron was to marry Catherine in the autumn and continues to dream up new boats and new top speeds. His heart belongs at sea with the *Albatros* and the waves. He dreams of furthering this sport, taking it to another level. Something tells me that somehow Bruno will make this dream a reality. Bruno, I owe you so much. I am forever thankful to you, my friend. You are The Master!

Hervé Jan and I continue to sail together when we can. He and his partner Kinny have bought a large farm on the west coast of Australia. Hervé has actually just signed up for his eighth voyage around the world.

Gilles Chiorri is working on many different projects. Gilles finished second overall in the 2002 Solitaire de Figaro, a result that will definitely help his aspirations.

Yann Eliès' wife gave birth to a baby boy shortly after our arrival. They named him Titouan after Titouan Lamazou, the winner of the first Vendée Globe race and advocate of the Jules Verne record. Yann continued his Figaro campaign through 2002 winning the final stage. I was driving through France listening to a commentary of Yann's fight to the finish on the radio. It was a great experience – I was in the car yelling 'go Yanno, go!'

Ronan le Goff. After the finish Ronnie made a quick dash to Brazil to buy a home among the palm trees in Bahia, Salvador. Two weeks later he was working towards another Jules Verne like Hervé. This project had Ronnie based in the UK for a period whilst I was there and we shared a house together for the summer, which was great.

Vladimir Dzalba-Lyndis continued with *Orange* as skipper. The boat was sold and changed her branding in the autumn and I guess Vlad hit the beach. I went sailing for a day with him onboard *Orange* mid-summer during a brief promotional tour in the UK. It was great to see them both again.

Jean-Baptiste Epron went to work immediately after the finish, piecing together the footage that he captured during our voyage to make a video piece. His photos still circulate the world giving people a taste of the things we saw. J-B is a Parisian but he bought Hervé's house near the Brittany coast after Hervé moved to Australia. J-B continues to decorate the latest and greatest French racing boats through his graphic art company.

Philippe Péché (Pépêche) returned to Perth in Western Australia where he works on many different projects. He is a performance sailing consult-ant and manages such programmes as sail co-ordinator for the famous *Foncia* 60-foot/18-metre Tri Grand Prix Team. Pépêche also has two high performance 30-foot/9-metre catamarans in Perth where he coaches and from where he races.

Benoit Briand continues to race on the 60-foot/18-metre trimaran circuit and develop sails. He will be sailing around the world with Ronnie and Hervé again this winter as a sail co-ordinator, developing high-tec fabrics for long distance ocean racing. I have spoken a few times to B-B and we communicate by email. He seems as relaxed and happy as ever.

Sébastien Josse secured a big sponsor and a boat shortly after our arrival, enabling him to focus fully on the 2004 Vendée Globe race. J-B applied the decoration to Seb's new boat for the Route du Rhum, the solo transatlantic race that I was also to compete in, in a different class. An already accomplished solo sailor, this was Jo Jo's next step towards the Vendée and my first. Sadly Jo Jo's mast failed and tumbled into the sea hours after the start of the race. I remember at the start looking for Seb in the distance, then he was gone. I received the news that night at sea and my heart sank.

Yves le Blévec went on to work with Jo Jo's campaign assisting with some modifications made to the boat, not the mast. I couldn't think of better hands to place my new boat in. It was great to spend time prior to the start with Jo Jo and Yves. We caught up one night to reminisce over a few beers. Wherever Yves is today, he is probably covered in carbon fibre dust, without a single complaint.

Florent Chastel went on to join the 60-foot tri Grand Prix circuit. He lives in the South of France which means more travelling but now by plane or train. I would not be surprised if I payed him a visit one day to find him running his own rigging business. I would definitely transfer all my work towards him if he ever does. When I think of Florent, one particular memory jumps out at me; on about day 40 after all the hot chocolate had long been finished, Florent appeared with a few satchels that he had been saving for myself and Vlad who were the only ones onboard that did not drink coffee or tea. It's hard to describe what that means when you have so little of life's normalities for so long.

There are many other acts of friendship, kindness and bravery that I have not been able to squeeze into this book but they shall remain strong memories to those of us that were there sharing together the discomfort, the wet, the aches, the stress, the excitement, the thrill, the relief and the elation.

Orange went on sailing throughout the summer of 2002 on promotional work. She missed the Round Britain and Ireland record by minutes. Sadly her mast finally broke into three pieces and sank to the bottom of the Mediterranean Sea. Shortly after that she changed her branding to support Castorama and B&Q, two subsidiaries of Kingfisher plc. Kingfisher plc was to continue its sponsorship support of Ellen MacArthur who, after securing a remarkable second place in the 2000–2001 Vendée Globe solo race around the world non-stop, had decided to put in for a Jules Verne attempt. This would be *Orange's* third lap of the planet as she was created to compete in the first edition of The Race as *Innovation Explorer*, when she came in second.

It would seem logical that I too should join Ellen's team for the attempt as Ellen and I are two skippers of The Offshore Challenges Sailing Team but I have just decided to concentrate all my focus and energy towards my own Vendée Globe campaign.

As for me, Nick Moloney, it had been a life-long dream for my mum to go shopping in Paris so we made the journey to the world's most beautiful city to fulfill that one for her. During the shopping spree we took a little time out to pay a visit to the French National Maritime Museum, the latest home of the Trophée Jules Verne, and I showed my parents what the fuss was all about, the reason for the months spent at sea. It was strange to see that canoe body suspended on its magnetic field again, some seven years after I promised myself to one day be part of it.

A few months later a very nervous solo sailor left the port of St-Malo on 9 November 2002 on a mission to race across the Atlantic Ocean. Forty-nine competitors started the Route du Rhum that year and sailed into the teeth of a hurricane: 22 boats and sailors emerged on the other side; 21 made the finish in Guadeloupe. Amongst that 21 was a solo Australian. I had not only become the first Australian to finish that race but I won my class taking nearly two days off the previous course record. I had moved another step closer to fulfilling my third offshore sailing goal.

Silence still wakes me in the night wondering what has happened. Have we lost the wind? Are we flying a hull? Then I realise that I'm in a real bed in a real house, on terra fima.

I paid our orange cat a visit the other day, just to say hello. Tomorrow at the Paris Boat Show our team will get together to be officially awarded that magnificent prize. It will be the first time that I have seen some of the guys since leaving Brest at the finish. Wearing black silk gloves we will take that chrome canoe body, each team member with one hand supporting its weight. We will place the canoe body over the magnetic field and slowly move our hands away leaving it floating in space above the magnetic base that now has another 13 names freshly engraved into its surface. What a moment that will be. The only ones absent from the occasion will be Pépêche and of course 'Maxi Catamaran Orange'. We will be thinking of you both.

I guess this is where I sign off... I have already written the page overleaf, in fact I wrote it at sea. It's a message for my team mates written by me and out of respect for them it is in French with no English translation. When I arrive back from the show tomorrow night, I will sit behind my computer and type two more words...

THE END!

Postscript

Pendant 64 jours, notre monde, c'est un bateau! Un bateau orange! Le chef Bruno et 12 indiens traversent les grands océans nord-sud-est-ouest. Un tour du monde à la voile, c'est une expérience extraordinaire. Le ciel bleu, les nuages, les poissons, le chaud, le froid, l'autoroute du grand sud, les tempêtes, les grands caps à laisser à bâbord, les grosses vagues, les glaces, les albatros, les étoiles, la lune... bref: la vie en mer.

Merci à Orange d'avoir cru en nos rêves!

Merci ma famille et mes amis pour votre soutien, pour vos prières et votre attente.

Merci à l'équipe de communication et à tous les gens qui nous ont suivis.

Merci l'équipe à terre de nous avoir donné l'opportunité de partir, surtout après le démâtage.

Merci Bruno de m'avoir pris dans l'équipe et merci pour les leçons en mer. Tu es le meilleur professeur!

Merci à l'équipage pour la bonne entente, pour l'ambiance, et pour avoir accepté un 'glaouich' à bord. Grand Merci les amis, pour toujours!

Merci le bateau de nous avoir ramenés à la maison sains et saufs.

Salut les Gars,

Nick

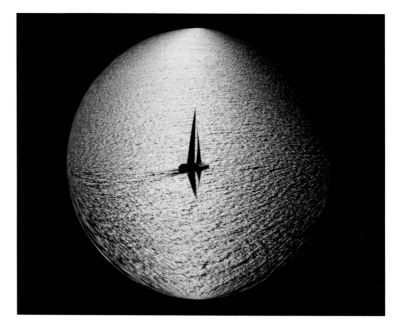

Index

Start/Finish

NORTH ATLANTIC OCEAN

NORTH PACIFIC OCEAN

Orange's circumnavigation
2nd March - 5th May 2002

64 days, 8 hours, 37 minutes and 45 seconds
This World Speed Record survived 6 attempts and stood for 701 days

Day 10

SOUTH A
OCE

SOUTH PACIFIC OCEAN

Day 40

SOUTHERN OCEAN

SOUTH